Enheduana

Enheduana: Princess, Priestess, Poetess offers the first comprehensive biography of Enheduana, daughter of Sargon of Agade and one of the most intriguing, yet elusive, women from antiquity.

Royal princess, priestess, and alleged author, Enheduana deserves as much attention as her martial relatives. A crucial contributor to her father's military ambitions, Enheduana nonetheless wielded religious and economic power, as evidenced by primary and secondary sources. Even more interestingly, Enheduana remained alive in the cultural memory of those who came after her, so much so that works attributed to her were integrated into the scribal curriculum centuries after her death. This book aims to situate Enheduana in her own historical context, allowing readers to gain a better understanding of this enigmatic figure, her roles as princess, priestess, and poetess, and the tumultuous times in which she lived.

This book is suitable for students, scholars, and the general reader interested in the history of the ancient Near East, ancient literature, and women in the ancient world.

Alhena Gadotti is Professor of History and Assistant Dean for the College of Liberal Arts at Towson University, Maryland, US. An expert in Sumerian literary texts and Old Babylonian school education, Professor Gadotti has also published on women's history, emotions, and intertextuality. Her most recent book, *Living and Dying in Mesopotamia* (co-authored with Dr Alexandra Kleinerman), was released in 2023.

Routledge Ancient Biographies

Herod, 2nd edition
King of the Jews and Friend of the Romans
Peter Richardson and Amy Marie Fisher

L. Munatius Plancus, 2nd edition
Serving and Surviving in the Roman Revolution
Thomas H. Watkins

Agrippa II
The Last of the Herods
David M. Jacobson

Galen
A Thinking Doctor in Imperial Rome
Vivian Nutton

Cyrus the Great
A Biography of Kingship
Lynette Mitchell

Tutankhamun
A Biography
Martin Bommas

Enheduana
Princess, Priestess, Poetess
Alhena Gadotti

To find out more about this series, visit: https://www.routledge.com/Routledge-Ancient-Biographies/book-series/ANCIENTBIOS

Enheduana
Princess, Priestess, Poetess

Alhena Gadotti

LONDON AND NEW YORK

First published 2025
by Routledge
4 Park Square, Milton Park, Abingdon, Oxon OX14 4RN

and by Routledge
605 Third Avenue, New York, NY 10158

Routledge is an imprint of the Taylor & Francis Group, an informa business

© 2025 Alhena Gadotti

The right of Alhena Gadotti to be identified as author of this work has been
asserted in accordance with sections 77 and 78 of the Copyright, Designs
and Patents Act 1988.

All rights reserved. No part of this book may be reprinted or reproduced or
utilised in any form or by any electronic, mechanical, or other means, now
known or hereafter invented, including photocopying and recording, or in
any information storage or retrieval system, without permission in writing
from the publishers.

Trademark notice: Product or corporate names may be trademarks or
registered trademarks, and are used only for identification and explanation
without intent to infringe.

British Library Cataloguing-in-Publication Data
A catalogue record for this book is available from the British Library

Library of Congress Cataloging-in-Publication Data
Names: Gadotti, Alhena, author.
Title: Enheduana: princess, priestess, poetess / Alhena Gadotti.
Description: London; New York: Routledge, 2025. |
Series: Routledge ancient biographies |
Includes bibliographical references and index.
Identifiers: LCCN 2024060172 (print) | LCCN 2024060173 (ebook) |
ISBN 9781032641133 (hardback) | ISBN 9781032641140 (paperback) |
ISBN 9781032641164 (ebook)
Subjects: LCSH: Enheduanna. | Enheduanna–Influence. |
Assyro-Babylonian poetry–History and criticism. | Babylonia–History. |
Women–Iraq–Babylonia–Biography. | Babylonia–Kings and
rulers–Biography.
Classification: LCC DS73.25 .G34 2025 (print) | LCC DS73.25 (ebook) |
DDC 935/.501092–dc23/eng/20250320
LC record available at https://lccn.loc.gov/2024060172
LC ebook record available at https://lccn.loc.gov/2024060173

ISBN: 978-1-032-64113-3 (hbk)
ISBN: 978-1-032-64114-0 (pbk)
ISBN: 978-1-032-64116-4 (ebk)

DOI: 10.4324/9781032641164

Typeset in Times New Roman
by Deanta Global Publishing Services, Chennai, India

Mama

Contents

Acknowledgments	*ix*
List of Abbreviations	*xi*
List of Figures	*xiii*

1 Introduction   1

Evidence for Enheduana   *2*
The Sargonic Period: Documents, Architecture, Art   *4*
Book Purpose and Structure   *9*
Conventions   *9*
Notes   *11*

2 The Sargonic Period: History and Legacy   15

The Historical Context   *15*
The Memory of the Kings of Agade   *27*
Notes   *30*

3 Enheduana the Princess   36

Notes   *43*

4 Enheduana the Priestess   47

Introduction   *47*
The City of Ur   *47*
Mesopotamian Religion: Sumerian and Akkadian   *52*
The Origins of Enheduana's Office   *54*
Enheduana's Installation   *55*
The Office of High Priestess   *55*
   Religious Duties   *56*

viii   *Contents*

> *The Disk of Enheduana   59*
> *Political Role(s)   63*
> *Economic Roles   64*
> *Daily Life: The ŋipar at Ur   66*
> *Daily Life: Enheduana's Experience   70*
> *Notes   73*

5   Enheduana the Poetess   82

> *Introduction   82*
> *A (Very) Brief History of the Scholarship   83*
> *On Mesopotamian Genre   85*
> *Authorship in Cuneiform Literature   85*
> *The Compositions Attributed to Enheduana: Context,*
> *   Summary, Analysis   89*
> *The Old Babylonian Sumerian Scribal Curriculum   94*
> *The Case of Ninshatapada   96*
> *Enheduana as Traditional Character   100*
> *Notes   104*

6   Conclusion   112

> *Notes   114*

Index   *115*

Acknowledgments

This book would not have been possible without the support of friends and colleagues who assisted me as I wrote it while also navigating a new job as Assistant Dean at my institution.

First and foremost, my heartfelt thanks to Dr Alexandra Kleinerman, who read and edited several iterations of this volume. Her extraordinary editing skills and acumen contributed extensively to making this book what it is.

Second, I must thank Dr Karen Eskow, Professor and Associate Dean of the College of Liberal Arts, Towson University, for her support. Our daily walks were a breath of fresh air as I tried to figure things out—with the book and with my new responsibilities as Assistant Dean. She also often reminded me that research is an integral part of what we do, even as administrators.

Many thanks, too, to Marcia Adams of Routledge, who contacted me with an idea I did not think I could bring to fruition and provided a sounding board as I considered the reviewers' feedback.

Speaking of the two anonymous reviewers: their comments were invaluable. I want to extend my gratitude to both, as they provided additional references and new avenues of investigation. The expert in the Sargonic period was instrumental in helping me reconfigure some sections of the book and rewrite one of the chapters. Space constraints (50,000 words) did not allow me to incorporate everything they recommended, but I learned a lot from them.

The Dean's Office in the College of Liberal Arts, Towson University, also supported me as I completed this work. My colleagues allowed me to carve out time to proofread the book, and to work on the map and the index. While most of the writing occurred away from the office, their flexibility was very much appreciated. Thank you, Melanie, for making my schedule work!

I am deeply grateful also to Dean Chris Chulos, who assisted me in getting a grant to finance some of the illustrations that accompany the book.

Special thanks go to the Trustees of the British Museum, the Musée du Louvre, the Museum of Archaeology and Anthropology, University of Philadelphia, and to Prof. Lorenzo Nigro, Professor, Institute for Oriental Studies, Sapienza University, Rome, for providing said illustrations. And to Dr Paporn Thebpanya, Professor, Department of Geography and Environmental Planning, Towson University, for designing the map for the volume.

x *Acknowledgments*

This book is dedicated to my mom, Marilena Rigon. I would not be where I am today if it weren't for her, and not just because she... well, she is my mom! Her unconditional love, unwavering support, and, at times, unrelenting nagging have been the foundations upon which I built my career. Always allowing me to make my own choices and my own mistakes, she has also lent an ear or a hand, and, when needed, a push or a kick. She truly is not just a mother, but a wise (old) woman and a lifelong teacher.

As always: Grazie mama!

Abbreviations

AAAS	*Les Annales Archéologiques Arabes Syriennes: Revue d'archéologie et d'histoire*
AAE	*Arabian Archaeology and Epigraphy*
Adab	*Yang Zhi, Sargonic Inscriptions from Adab*
AfO	*Archiv für Orientforschung*
AION	*Annali dell'Istituto Universitario Orientale di Napoli*
AJA	*American Journal of Archaeology*
AJNES	*ARAMAZD: Armenian Journal of Near Eastern Studies*
Akkadica	*Akkadica. Périodique bimestriel de la Fondation Assyriologique Georges Dossin*
AP3A	*Archaeological Papers of the American Anthropological Association*
AUAM	*Tablets in the collections of the Andrews University Archaeological Museum*
BM	*Museum siglum of the British Museum, London*
BSA	*Bulletin of Sumerian Agriculture*
CBS	*Museum siglum of the University Museum in Philadelphia (Catalogue of the Babylonian Section)*
CSSH	*Comparative Studies in Society and History*
CUSAS	*Cornell University Studies in Assyriology and Sumerology*
DABIR	*Digital Archive of Brief Notes & Iran Review*
DWJ	*Distant Worlds Journal*
Geophys. J. Int.	*International Journal of Geophysics*
HAR	*Hungarian Assyriological Review*
Hist. Rel.	*History of Religions*
ISET	*S. Kramer/M. Çig/H. Kizilyay, Istanbul Arkeoloji Müzelerinde bulunan Sumer edebi tablet ve parcalari (Sumerian Literary Tablets and Fragments in the Archaeological Museum of Istanbul), I/Il, (Ankara 1969/1976)*
KASKAL	*KASKAL. Rivista di storia, ambiente, e culture del vicino oriente antico*

xii *Abbreviations*

JANEH	*Journal of Ancient Near Eastern History*
JANES	*Journal of the Ancient Near Eastern Society*
JAOS	*Journal of the American Oriental Society*
JCS	*Journal of Cuneiform Studies*
JESHO	*Journal for the Economic and Social History of the Orient*
MLQ	*Modern Language Quarterly*
Orb. Litt.	*Orbis Litterarum*
OrNS	*Orientalia. Nova Series*
PBLJ	*Poetry Birmingham Literary Journal*
Proc. Br. Ac.	*Proceedings of the British Academy*
QuadSem	*Quaderni di Semitistica*
RA	*Revue d'Assyriologie*
Relig. Compass	*Religious Compass*
Riv. Stor. Econ.	*Rivista di Storia Economica*
RIME	*The Royal Inscriptions of Mesopotamia, Early Periods*
RlA	*Reallexikon der Assyriologie und vorderorientalische Archäologie*
SemRom	*Seminari Romani di Cultura Greca*
U	*Find siglum, Ur (London/Philadelphia/Baghdad)*
WO	*Die Welt des Orients*
ZA	*Zeitschrift für Assyriologie und vorderasiatische Archäologie*

Figures

	Map of the Region with Toponyms Mentioned in the Book: Created by Paporn Thebpanya	xiv
2.1	Victory Stele of Naram-Sin, Sargonic Period. From Susa. Courtesy of the Musée du Louvre	25
4.1	Sb 2/6053. Drawing of the Stele of Sargon, Sargonic Period. From Susa. Courtesy of Lorenzo Nigro	48
4.2	Disk of Enheduana, Sargonic Period. From Ur. Courtesy of the University of Pennsylvania Museum of Archaeology and Anthropology, Philadelphia	60
4.3	Disk of Enheduana before Reconstruction, Sargonic Period. From Ur. Courtesy of the University of Pennsylvania Museum of Archaeology and Anthropology, Philadelphia	61
4.4	Statuette of Enanatuma, Old Babylonian Period. From Ur. Courtesy of the University of Pennsylvania Museum of Archaeology and Anthropology, Philadelphia	62
4.5	Plan of the Ur Ziggurat Complex, Ur. © The Trustees of the British Museum	67
4.6	Plan of the ŋipar at Ur. © The Trustees of the British Museum	68

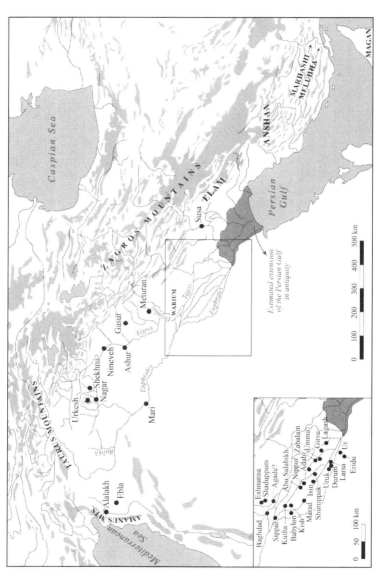

Map of the Region with Toponyms Mentioned in the Book: Created by Paporn Thebpanya

1 Introduction

The Great Revolt against Naram-Sin might have been one of the most harrowing events in the long life of Enheduana, daughter of King Sargon and high priestess of the moon god Nanna/Sin at Ur (mod. Tell el-Muqayyar). In a composition attributed to her, *Ninmeshara* ("Queen of all Divine Powers," also known by its modern titles *The Exaltation of Inana* or *Inana B*), Enheduana recounts the time when a group of southern Mesopotamian cities rebelled against her family's rulership. Dedicated to Inana, the Sumerian goddess of warfare and sex, *Inana B* extols Inana's supremacy over all other deities.[1] Embedded in the hymn is an appeal to Nanna, Inana's father. Enheduana hopes he will intercede with An, the sky god, so she will be freed of Lugal-Ane, one of the rebel leaders:

> This fate of mine, Sin, Lugalane—
> do speak to An about him so that An might redress the matter.
> Right now, do speak to An about him so that An might redress the matter.
> This fate (of mine), Lugalane: the woman (= Inana) will remove it.
> (After all,) mountains and floods lay at her feet.
> This woman is exalted, she makes entire cities tremble,
> Stand up (Sin), so that she shall have mercy on me.[2]

This is not literary hyperbole. Sometime during the reign of Naram-Sin (c. 2253–2198 BCE), Enheduana's great-nephew and the fourth ruler of the Sargonic Dynasty, the people of southern Mesopotamia selected two locals and elevated them to kingship. Iphur-Kish became king of Kish and Amar-girid king of Uruk.[3] Together, they formed a coalition that included cities in the northern and southern parts of the Mesopotamian alluvium (c. 2230 BCE).[4] This was an outright rebellion against the Sargonic yoke, the first one since the reign of Rimush, Sargon's successor, almost half a century earlier (c. 2276 BCE). Naram-Sin emerged victorious, and more than 95,000 people—most likely soldiers—were killed, including the leaders of the revolt.[5] As for Lugal-Ane, who had proclaimed himself king of Ur, he is attested only

DOI: 10.4324/9781032641164-1

2 *Enheduana*

in the literary tradition, but this does not mean he was not a historical figure.[6] Among all rebel kings, he was perfectly positioned to threaten not just the Sargonic power in the south but also Enheduana's position and her life.

So epochal was the Great Revolt that it had lasting repercussions. Two are worth mentioning. Naram-Sin proclaimed himself to be a living god, something that no Mesopotamian ruler had done before. Furthermore, Naram-Sin's victory was not only commemorated in his royal inscriptions—and presumably in the accompanying art, most of which does not survive—but it was also incorporated in a literary text composed about the kings of Akkad, which continued to be copied generations after the dynasty's demise. The *Great Revolt Against Naram-Sin* survives in one contemporary school text and on tablets written about four centuries after the events they recount.[7] Already during the Sargonic period, therefore, this rebellion was the stuff of legends.[8]

Enheduana's alleged involvement in the Great Revolt highlights one of the most complex yet fascinating aspects of the period in which she lived. Numerous extant sources help us flesh out the political, social, and economic history of these turbulent times. Yet, several of these sources are literary in nature, even if they profess to recount historical events. Therefore, the modern scholar must sift carefully through them, paying close attention to their purpose, their function, and their original date of composition, often unknown.

Evidence for Enheduana

Contemporary evidence about Enheduana is scarce. Of almost 10,000 documents that survive from the Sargonic period (c. 2316–2163 BCE), only five mention her directly. These comprise inscriptions located on three-cylinder seals, one seal impression, and the alabaster Disk of Enheduana.

Of these items, four were discovered in Ur, either in or near the complex where Enheduana spent most of her life. The five that mention her directly are:

1) a lapis lazuli seal found in a private grave from the nearby cemetery. Its inscription identifies the seal's owner: "Enheduana, daughter of Sargon. Ilum-pa[lil] (is) her coiffeur";[9]
2) a mottle stone seal uncovered in the loose soil of the same cemetery. The seal belonged to Enheduana's estate manager, as the inscription tells us: "Adda, chief administrator/majordomo of Enheduana";[10]
3) the poorly preserved impression of a seal found in the loose upper soil of the cemetery. The legend reads: "[En]-he-[du]-ana [daughter of Sa]rgon. [x]-kitush-du, [the scri]be, (is) [h]er [servant]";[11]
4) a lapis lazuli seal of unknown provenance—but most likely from Ur. It reads: "Enheduana, daughter of Sargon. Sagadu, the scribe, (is) your servant";[12]

Introduction 3

5) the alabaster Disk of Enheduana. It was unearthed in several pieces on the floor of the Isin-Larsa period (c. 2025–1764 BCE) edifice that housed Enheduana's successors in the position of high priestess. On the front of the disk is a cultic scene most likely representing Enheduana supervising ritual matters. On its back is an inscription:

Enheduana, *zirru* of Nanna, wife of Nanna, daughter of Sargon, [king] of the world, in [the temple of the goddess Inan]a.ZA.ZA in Ur, made an altar (and) named it: 'altar, table of the god An' (or of the sky)'.[13]

This is it. There are no other documents mentioning Enheduana, and certainly no contemporaneous texts mentioning her achievements as an author. Yet, ancient scribes and modern scholars have connected her with several compositions. Without exception, these are preserved on tablets written between 100 and 500 years after her death. By nature, therefore, they are secondary sources. These compositions include:

a) **nin-me-šar₂-ra**, "Queen of All Divine Powers," attested exclusively on copies from the Old Babylonian period (c. 2004–1595 BCE). Enheduana speaks in the first person;

b) **in-nin ša₃-gur₄-ra**, "The Great-Hearted Mistress" (*Inana C*), attested exclusively on Old Babylonian copies. Enheduana speaks in the first person;

c) **e₂-u₆-nir**, "House of the Ziggurat" (*Temple Hymns*), attested only on Old Babylonian copies;

d) **e₂ ud-gin₇(?) e₃-a ki-en-gi-ra**, "House that Rises with the Sun over Sumer" (*Nanna C*), known from one Old Babylonian manuscript;

e) A composition whose title is unknown. It survives on a single tablet dated to the Third Dynasty of Ur (c. 2012–2004 BCE) or earlier;

f) **in-nin me-huš-a**, "Mistress of the Fearsome Divine Powers" (*Inana and Ebih*), known only from Old Babylonian copies. There is no consensus among scholars about Enheduana's authorship of this story;[14]

g) **me-a-am-ra me-e mu-u[n …]**, "To (My) Beloved I […]" (*Nanna B*), known from the same Old Babylonian manuscript that preserves *Nanna C*. In this case, too, scholarly consensus about Enheduana's authorship is lacking.

In sum, more compositions are attributed to Enheduana than there are contemporary documents mentioning her directly. More significantly, there are no coeval manuscripts of the works she allegedly authored. We will discuss the implications of this problem in Chapter 5.

Additional evidence for Enheduana's life comes from archaeological excavations. Crucial is the **ŋipar**/*gipāru* of the sanctuary of Nanna at Ur.

4 *Enheduana*

ŋipar/*gipāru* is typically translated as "cloister," a misnomer: the building was the high priestess's residence. It might have been constructed decades, if not centuries, before Enheduana became the office holder—sometime during the late part of the Early Dynastic period (c. 2900–2316 BCE).[15] It was most likely refurbished during Enheduana's lifetime and then reconfigured altogether in the Ur III period.[16] The building excavated in the 1920s had been repaired and refurbished in the early eighteenth century BCE by Eanedu, high priestess of Nanna and sister to the kings who ruled Ur at the time.

Enheduana likely spent most of her adult life in Ur. Contemporary archaeological remains exist for the city, and we will consider them in Chapter 4. Unfortunately, the capital of Sargon's reign, Agade, which might have been Enheduana's birthplace, has not been identified yet.

The Sargonic period was a time of great artistic innovation, especially during the so-called Classical Phase—the reigns of Naram-Sin and Shar-kali-sharri (c. 2197–2173 BCE).[17] Akkadian art includes the Disk of Enheduana. The female figure depicted on its front is depersonalized—as portraiture was in Mesopotamia. As such, it gives no inkling as to Enheduana's features. We will discuss its implications for understanding Enheduana's life further in Chapter 4.

The Sargonic Period: Documents, Architecture, Art

Extant sources for the reconstruction of the Sargonic period include written documents, archaeological remains, and art. While many are contemporary, others date from after the fall of the Sargonic Dynasty, which left a profound mark on the imagination of later people and their scholars.

Sargonic documents were written in either Sumerian or Akkadian, although bilingual texts exist. Sumerian, a language isolate, was in use from at least the early third millennium BCE, and maybe already in the fourth millennium.[18] Akkadian, a Semitic language, was used at least from the mid-third millennium BCE onwards.[19] Sumerian died out as a spoken language sometime around 2000 BCE, but Sumerian documents continued to be written until the first century CE.[20] Akkadian was in use throughout the second and first millennia BCE, when it was progressively replaced by Aramaic and eventually by Greek. Like Sumerian, Akkadian continued to be written down until the first century CE.[21]

The spread of Akkadian relates to the rise of the Sargonic Dynasty. Its founders likely originated from the northern part of southern Mesopotamia and spoke an East Semitic dialect we call (Old) Akkadian. They made "their own local variety of Akkadian … [the] bureaucratic language alongside Sumerian."[22] The terms "Sumerian" and "Akkadian" are somewhat misleading, however, as they provide the illusion of a neat linguistic demarcation that never really existed. Indeed, modern terminology "encompass[es] a variety of written dialects and languages, which may not reveal much about what was

Introduction 5

surely an assortment of spoken dialects."[23] Relatedly, written sources help us understand the nature of written Sumerian and Akkadian. The complexities of their spoken versions are lost to us, especially when considering the issue of alloglottography, wherein a text is written in a language that is different from how the text is read.[24]

Most Sargonic documents are administrative (approximately 8,000) and date largely to the Classical Sargonic Phase. Administrative texts have been found in private and public (institutional) archives.[25] They have been uncovered in southern Mesopotamia, where the activities of the Sargonic administration are best documented, and in northern Mesopotamia, the Diyala Region, and in the city of Susa (mod. Shush) in the Zagros Mountains.[26] Depending on their place of origin, Sargonic administrative documents were written either in Sumerian (in the south) or Akkadian (in the north). But the situation was fluid. The southern Mesag archive, for instance, includes several mixed-language texts.[27]

The main topics of administrative texts are agriculture and animal husbandry but also include military and commercial concerns.[28] These documents allow modern scholars to reconstruct the mechanisms enacted to run an increasingly vast and more complex state apparatus effectively. The changes evidenced in the physical shape of tablets and the cuneiform script highlight measures implemented by the central administration. In addition, administrative texts could carry a date. Important for reconstructing Sargonic history was the use of year names, a practice by which a year was named after an important event—for example, a military victory, a religious occurrence, or the enthronement of a new ruler. While year names—also attested on contracts—are ideologically charged, they can be mined for information. They do not help, however, in establishing a relative or absolute chronology of the Sargonic period, at least not yet.

Approximately 150 letters and as many legal texts further illustrate the inner workings of the administration and its justice system.[29] Sargonic letters are short communications written in Sumerian or Akkadian. Exchanged between administrators, they address border problems, legal issues, and matters of real estate, personnel (such as enslaved people and fugitives), and agriculture.[30] They are often difficult to understand, as we lack their context. Sargonic legal documents can be equally opaque.[31] Yet, they inform us about personal status, family law, criminal law, and international law at the time.[32] Many of these texts are land purchase contracts, but other transactions are attested.

Additionally, we possess incantations, votive inscriptions, seal inscriptions, and school texts.[33] Incantations belong to the realm of medicine and magic. Written mostly in Akkadian, they were used by specialists to avert the action of evil agents, to whom illness and ill fortune were attributed.[34] Votive or dedicatory inscriptions illustrate Sargonic religious practices. Typically written (in Sumerian or Akkadian) on portable objects for the health of wealthy individuals, they were dedicated to various deities and meant to

6 *Enheduana*

ensure a long and prosperous life for the dedicant.[35] Seal inscriptions (also in Sumerian or Akkadian) consist of basic information marking the identity of the seal owner, such as those of Enheduana's personnel.

School texts currently amount to almost 300.[36] Their purpose seems to have been the training of future members of the Sargonic administrative apparatus. The vast majority comes from the southern city of Girsu (mod. Telloh), but a significant corpus has been found at Gasur (mod. Yorghan Tepe) in northern Iraq.[37] School texts were written either in Sumerian or Akkadian. Sumerian ones are associated with the Sumerian south, where older practices, including the use of Sumerian, were retained even after the Sargonic conquest. In the northern cities, scribes were educated in Akkadian.[38] This was the language spoken there, and which the Sargonic rulers helped spread.

At present, little information exists about literary production, and it comes primarily from school texts.[39] While literary works, such as hymns to gods and temples and wisdom literature, are attested before and after the Sargonic period, no complete text has been uncovered that can be securely dated to this time. Only excerpts have been identified that could fall into these genre categories. Nevertheless, some school tablets preserve sections of narrative texts, divine hymns, proverbs, and riddles.[40]

Finally, for reconstructing the main events of the Sargonic period, we depend heavily on approximately 150 royal inscriptions commissioned by the rulers to celebrate their accomplishments. Of these documents, several are contemporaneous, but many are preserved only on copies made during the Old Babylonian period. Presumably, the copyists could still see the original statues and steles upon which these texts had first been inscribed.[41] Yet, most originals are lost to us.

Sargonic kings commissioned royal inscriptions in Sumerian, Akkadian, or both, thereby inserting themselves into a long tradition of Sumerian royal inscriptions dating back centuries. Yet, the new rulers also wanted their deeds narrated in their own language. Although not without considerable methodological problems, these inscriptions will guide much of the historical reconstruction offered in Chapter 2.

Secondary sources can help us understand certain aspects of the Sargonic period. Later compositions recast certain Sargonic kings into new and heroic roles, a process which must have begun shortly after the end of the dynasty— if not even under the Sargonic kings themselves.[42] Some of them received funerary offerings during the Third Dynasty of Ur, whose rulers positioned themselves as the ideological heirs of the kings of Agade.[43] These rituals must have played a role in keeping the names of the Sargonic rulers in the minds of the kings who followed. For better or worse, Sargon and Naram-Sin became models of kingship for future generations, hailed as the protagonists of a time long gone. Compositions about them were written well into the first millennium, 2,000 years after their deaths.[44]

Introduction 7

Furthermore, the names of the Sargonic rulers were incorporated into the Mesopotamian omen tradition, connected to the practice of divination—the prediction of the future through the observation of natural phenomena. Celestial divination and extispicy are particularly informative about the memory of the kings of Agade.[45] The former practice consisted of the observation of the movements of celestial bodies; the latter was the reading of sheep's entrails. Observations and their interpretations were collected in manuals used to train divination specialists.

While thousands of documents help us reconstruct numerous aspects of the Sargonic period, architectural evidence is hard to come by. Agade, the dynastic capital, has not been located. Furthermore, due to the significant building programs of subsequent rulers, the edifices erected and refurbished by the Sargonic kings were either destroyed already in antiquity or incorporated into later construction projects.[46] Yet, edifices have been unearthed in northern and southern Mesopotamia.

Monumental buildings have been discovered in imperial outposts such as Nagar (mod. Tell Brak) in northern Syria, where a palace and two religious and/or administrative buildings have been identified.[47] Particularly interesting is the so-called Palace of Naram-Sin, a massive building with a rectilinear plan arranged around a large central courtyard.[48] Its outer walls were thick and buttressed, with only one entrance situated on the western side. The local administration was concerned with security—unsurprisingly considering that they were an occupying force in a conquered land. Another monumental edifice has been identified at Shekhna (mod. Tell Leilan), also in northern Syria, and also under Sargonic occupation.[49]

A palace and a temple have been excavated at Urkesh (mod. Tell Mozan) in northern Syria. While the city remained independent, Sargonic influence must have been present.[50] The Sargonic occupational levels of the temple at Urkesh are not well attested. As such, not much can be concluded about the building, which might date back to the fourth millennium BCE.[51]

Finally, a massive complex in Eshnunna (mod. Tell Asmar) dates to the Sargonic period.[52] Labeled the Northern Palace, this edifice did not have a regular plan but developed as an adaptation of an earlier building.[53] Characterized by a complex drainage system, the edifice might have been a palace, or it might have been associated with the Abu Temple, located nearby.[54]

Domestic architecture has been identified at Eshnunna and Nippur (mod. Niffar) and displays continuity with previous practices.[55] This is also the case for Sargonic burials, which have thus far been uncovered only in a few sites, such as the cemetery at Ur. However, people were also buried underneath the floors of their houses, for instance at Nippur.[56] This practice is attested throughout Mesopotamian history.

Artistic evidence includes sculptures in the round, reliefs, steles, and glyptic art, consisting of decoration on cylinder seals.[57] Interpreting this evidence can be problematic, especially since modern scholars often lack the context of

8 *Enheduana*

the surviving art and the indigenous discourse about artistic typologies, which would explain the use, meaning, and ideological underpinnings of these items. Nevertheless, when carefully studied, and considered with other evidence, they can provide valuable insight.

While elements of continuity with the artistic production of the preceding Early Dynastic period exist, the Sargonic period was characterized by innovation. Artists concerned themselves more with "naturalistic details and carving styles, a development that we can observe in every genre of representation."[58] Moreover, closer attention was paid to the representation of the human figure.[59]

The Sargonic period was a time of innovation in statuary. Indeed, "Akkadian sculpture is considered the 'classical' sculpture of ancient Mesopotamia, its masterpieces among the most frequently reproduced and most intensively studied works from the entire ancient Near East."[60] Sculpture in the round, as well as reliefs and steles, were political instruments that helped Sargonic rulers strengthen their ideological control over conquered people.[61] This was conveyed not only through images and accompanying texts, but also the choice of material. Stone and metal ores had to be imported from abroad.[62] Diorite from Magan/Makkan (mod. Oman) deposits was a favorite, and its use in statuary allowed the Sargonic kings to display visible evidence of their far-reaching influence.

Metalwork statuary developed during this period and became an integral component of the Sargonic visual discourse. Artists invented the hollow-cast lost wax method.[63] Through a series of successive steps—including the use of two clay layers and a detailed wax layer—a clay mold was produced, upon which metal was poured.[64] A copper alloy was used for life-size statues, only two of which survive. In both cases, the craftsmanship of the artists is on full display. Like diorite, copper had to be imported from Oman.[65] As such, metal statues, too, were the physical embodiment of the Sargonic rulers' success at harnessing foreign materials, and, synecdochally, foreign lands.

Tradition and innovation characterized glyptic art—the largest extant artistic corpus of the Sargonic period. Motifs that had become popular during the Early Dynastic period continued to be used, including contest scenes, which depicted mythical beings locked in combat, and banquet scenes that show individuals sharing a meal.[66] Yet, new designs emerged, reflecting the beliefs and preferences of the Sargonic elite—for instance, mythological scenes and daily life vignettes.[67]

When compared to other epochs, the Sargonic period is not one of the best-documented. Evidence is unevenly distributed diachronically and geographically. In addition, modern scholars tend to rely on royal inscriptions and other ideologically charged texts to reconstruct sequences of events—a dangerous practice. The kings of Agade tell us only what they wanted their people and their gods to know, and little else. Furthermore, "reading" building projects

Introduction 9

and artistic pieces presents challenges. Despite these obstacles, however, an adequate portrayal of the time when Enheduana lived will emerge from a careful examination of the evidence.

Book Purpose and Structure

When I was first approached to write a biography of Enheduana, I was skeptical of its feasibility. Sources are limited, and the information they provide is skewed. This is true of Enheduana and of the times when she lived. This does not mean that such an endeavor should not be undertaken.[68] And it has, as Enheduana has fascinated scholars and non-scholars alike for decades. Past works on Enheduana have focused on her role in the history of literature.[69] Particularly important have been contributions wherein scholars have attempted to situate Enheduana in the landscape of early Mesopotamian literary traditions and have used varied methods to evaluate her literary production.[70]

I have chosen a different approach for this monograph. I aim to situate my discussion of Enheduana's authorship within the broader historical context by discussing the times in which she lived (Chapter 2), what her life as a royal princess might have entailed (Chapter 3), and the religious, political, and economic ramifications of her role as high priestess of Nanna at Ur (Chapter 4).

Like others have done before, I, too, discuss her literary contributions (Chapter 5), but I do so by examining Old Babylonian scribal education. This was the environment that produced all but one of the manuscripts in which the compositions attributed to her are preserved. This approach nuances our understanding of Enheduana's literary contributions. Specifically, the argument of this book is that Enheduana was *not* the author of the compositions attributed to her. Rather, in the Old Babylonian scribal milieu, she became a traditional character and therefore a suitable foil to provide authorship to compositions used in scribal schools. This does not deny Enheduana's authorship altogether. Indeed, Old Babylonian scribes would not have chosen her as a model for authorship if she had not been renowned for her literary opus. However, her work, which might have been composed in Sumerian *and* Akkadian, is currently lost to us. Chapter 6 concludes and summarizes the main arguments of this book.

Conventions

In a book such as this, a few words about conventions and terminology are essential. First, the time when Enheduana lived is called the Old Akkadian period, the Akkadian period, or the Sargonic period. These are modern labels. The first refers to the phase of the Akkadian language that was in use at this

10   *Enheduana*

time—the earliest currently documented. The second derives from the notion that the dynasty ruled from the city of Agade in the land of Akkad. The third comes from Sargon, the founder of the dynasty, from whom all successive rulers descended. In this book, I privilege Sargonic, but others may appear in citations.

Second, Mesopotamia is originally a Greek term, nowadays generally understood as "between the rivers," the Tigris River to the east and the Euphrates River to the west.[71] These names, too, are Greek; the Tigris was called **Idig(i)na** (Sumerian) and *Idiqlat* (Akkadian), while the Euphrates was known as **Buranuna** (Sumerian) and *Purattum* (Akkadian). Incidentally, the concept of Mesopotamia as the land between two rivers goes back to Naram-Sin himself, who claimed in his royal inscriptions to be the *kibrāt arba'i*, "king of the four quarters (of the known world)" or "king of the four riverbanks."

Mesopotamia corresponds to part of the modern Middle East (or ancient Near East), a region situated at the intersection of three continents: Asia, Africa, and Europe. This territory is equivalent to Iraq, northern and central Syria, western Iran, and southeastern Türkiye. The area north of Baghdad is called northern or Upper Mesopotamia, as well as Assyria (from the city of Ashur). The territories south of Baghdad are known as southern or Lower Mesopotamia. This region is also referred to by modern scholars as Babylonia (from the city of Babylon), as well as Sumer and Akkad. The last two are ancient designations referring respectively to the southernmost part of southern Mesopotamia and its northern equivalent. In this book, I mostly use northern and southern Mesopotamia, but familiarity with the other terms is needed.

Third, the people who lived in Mesopotamia during Enheduana's lifetime used two main languages: Sumerian and Akkadian. In this volume, Sumerian terms are represented in **bold**, while Akkadian terms are in *italics*. These two languages, and others used by the people of Mesopotamia, were written in cuneiform, a writing system developed at the end of the fourth millennium BCE in the context of the temple of Inana and An at Uruk (mod. Warka), in southern Mesopotamia.[72] Cuneiform is a logo-syllabic script, in which a grapheme, or sign, can represent a syllable or a word. Through the process of transliteration, modern scholars put cuneiform signs into syllables represented by the Latin alphabet. These sequences are then normalized so that we go from 𒂗𒃶𒇻𒌌𒀭𒈾 to **en-he₂-du₁₁-an-na** to Enheduana. The reader should not be surprised if some terms, whether in Sumerian or Akkadian, look unfamiliar.

Fourth, I opted not to use special characters for ease of reading. Therefore, the sound /sh/ (as in shop or ship), typically rendered as š in transliteration, is conveyed through "sh." Thus, I use Shar-kali-sharri and not Šar-kali-šarri. I also do not mark long and extra-long vowels in the normalization. As such, the name of the founder of the dynasty is consistently written as Sargon, and

Introduction 11

not *Šarru-ukīn* or *Šarru-kēn*. Also, according to Assyriological practices, in a translated text, square brackets […] indicate a break in the original document. The lost portion can at times be reconstructed based on parallel passages. Parentheses ( ) are used to provide clarifying information.

Finally, a note on Agade: the name of the city came to describe the kingdom governed by the Sargonic rulers. It is transliterated differently by modern scholars, so that the reader might encounter Akkad, Akkade, Accad, and Agade in the literature. In this book, Agade designates the city, while Akkad refers to the land.[73]

The minutiae out of the way, let us turn to Enheduana's times.

Notes

1 Sophus Helle, *Enheduana: The Complete Poems of the World's First Author* (New Haven & London: Yale University Press, 2023), 4.
2 *Ninmeshara*, ll. 74–80. Unless otherwise indicated, translations are my own.
3 RIME 2.1.4.6 col. i, ll. 1′-9′.
4 Walther Sallaberger and Ingo Schrakamp, *ARCANE III: History and Philology* (Turnhout: Brepols Publishers, 2015), 109.
5 Ingo Schrakamp, "The Kingdom of Akkad: A View from Within," in *The Oxford History of the Ancient Near East: Volume I: From the Beginnings to Old Kingdom Egypt and the Dynasty of Akkad*. ed. by Karen Radner, Nadine Moeller and Daniel T. Potts (Oxford: Oxford University Press, 2020), 612–85, 632–3; RIME 2.1.4.6 in Douglas R. Frayne, *Sargonic and Gutian Periods* (2234–2113 BC) (Toronto/Buffalo/London: University of Toronto Press, 1993), 103–8.
6 Aage Westenholz, 'The Old Akkadian Period: History and Culture', in *Mesopotamien: Akkade-Zeit und Ur III-Zeit*, by Walther Sallaberger and Aage Westenholz. (Fribourg/Göttingen: Universitätsverlag/Vandenhoeck & Ruprecht, 1999), 17–117, 53–4; Joan Goodnick Westenholz, *Legends of the Kings of Akkade* (Winona Lake, IN: Eisenbrauns, 1997), 223; Michael Haul, *Stele und Legende. Untersuchungen zu den keilschriftlichen Erzählwerken über die Könige von Akkade* (Göttinger: Universitätsverlag Göttingen, 2009), 38–40.
7 Westenholz, *Legends*, 221.
8 Westenholz, *Legends*, 223–9.
9 RIME 2.1.1.2203 = U. 8988 = BM 12572, reproduced in Sidney Babcock and Erhan Tamur, *She Who Wrote: Enheduanna and Women of Mesopotamia ca. 3400–2000 BC* (New York: The Morgan Library and Museum, 2022), 175, no. 56.
10 RIME 2.1.1.2004 = U. 9178 = IM 4221.
11 RIME 2.1.1.2005 = U. 11684 = BM 123688, reproduced in Babcock and Tamur, *She Who Wrote*, 174, no. 55.
12 Babcock and Tamur, *She Who Wrote*, 176, no. 57.
13 RIME 2.1.1.16 = U 6612 = CBS 16665
14 Gina Kostantopoulos, 'The Many Lives of Enheduana: Identity, Authorship and the "World's First Poet"', in *Powerful Women in the Ancient World: Perception and (Self)Presentation*, ed. by Kerstin Droß-Krüpe and Sebastian Fink (Munster: Zaphon, 2021), 57–76, 60 and fn. 15.
15 Penelope N. Weadock, 'The Giparu at Ur', *Iraq* 37, no. 2 (1975): 101–28, 105–6.
16 Weadock, 'Giparu at Ur', 106–7.
17 Pierre Amiet, *L'art du Agade au Musée du Louvre* (Paris: Editions de Musées Nationaux, 1976); Melissa Eppihimer, *Exemplars of Kingship. Art, Tradition, and the Legacy of the Akkadians* (Oxford: Oxford University Press, 2019).

12   *Enheduana*

18 Christopher Woods, 'The Earliest Mesopotamian Writing', in *Visible Language. Inventions of Writing in the Ancient Middle East and Beyond*, ed. by Christopher Woods (Chicago: The Oriental Institute of the University of Chicago, 2010), 33–50.

19 Manfred Krebernik, 'Mesopotamian Myths at Ebla: ARET 5, 6 and ARET 5, 7', in *Literature and Literary Language at Ebla*, ed. by Pelio Fronzaroli (Florence: Università di Firenze, 1992), 72–86.

20 Piotr Michalowski, 'The Lives of the Sumerian Language', in *Margins of Writing, Origins of Cultures*, ed. by Seth L. Sanders (Chicago, IL: The University of Chicago Press, 2006), 159–84.

21 Markham J. Geller, 'The Last Wedge', *ZA* 87 (1997): 43–95.

22 C. Jay Crisostomo, 'Sumerian and Akkadian Language Contact', in *A Companion to Ancient Near Eastern Languages*, ed. by Rebecca Hasselback-Andee (Hoboken, NJ: John Wiley & Sons, 2020), 403–20, 410.

23 Crisostomo, 'Sumerian and Akkadian', 404.

24 E.g., Crisostomo, 'Sumerian and Akkadian', 407–8.

25 Benjamin R. Foster, 'Archives and Record-Keeping in Sargonic Mesopotamia', *ZA* 72 (1982): 1–27.

26 Foster, 'Archives and Record-Keeping', 3.

27 Ekaterina Markina, 'Akkadian of the Me-ség Archive', *Babel und Bibel* 6 (2012): 169–88.

28 Foster, 'Archives and Record-Keeping', 7–12.

29 Schrakamp, 'A View from Within', 616; Claus Wilcke, 'Early Dynastic and Sargonic Periods', in *A History of Ancient Near Eastern Law*, ed. by Raymond Westbrook, 2 vols. (Leiden/Boston, Brill, 2003), 141–81.

30 Piotr Michalowski, *Letters from Early Mesopotamia* (Atlanta, GA: SBL Press, 1993), 19–51; Massimo Maiocchi, 'The Old Akkadian Letter Corpus: New Interpretation and a Possible Addition', *Akkadica* 137 (2016): 183–93.

31 Wilcke, 'Early Dynastic and Sargonic Periods', 141–81

32 An international treaty survives that was ratified between Naram-Sin and an Elamite ruler (Walter Hinz, 'Elams Verlag mit Narām-Sîn von Akkade', *ZA* 58 (1967): 66–96).

33 Schrakamp, 'A View from Within', 616.

34 Examples in Sumerian also exist in school texts; see Nicholas L. Kraus, *Scribal Education in the Sargonic Period* (Boston/Leiden: Brill, 2020), 136–7.

35 Some of these inscriptions were copied by pupils as they trained in scribal schools. See Kraus, *Scribal Education*, 124–6.

36 Kraus, *Scribal Education*, 5. This number is ever changing. See, e.g., Hanan A. Alessawee and Abdulmukrem M. Alezzi, 'A Sargonic Learner Tablet with an Invocation of the Goddess Nisaba', *JCS* 73 (2021): 3–8; Jana Matuszak and Hanan Abd Alhamza Alessawe, 'A Sargonic Exercise Tablet Listing "Places of Inanna" and Personal Names', *JCS* 76 (2024): 27–52.

37 Kraus, *Scribal Education*, 9.

38 Kraus, *Scribal Education*, 164–8, 177–81.

39 Kraus, *Scribal Education*, 112–38.

40 Kraus, *Scribal Education*, 128–32.

41 Schrakamp, 'A View from Within', 616.

42 Benjamin R. Foster, *The Age of Agade. Inventing Empire in Ancient Mesopotamia* (Milton Park, UK/New York: Routledge, 2015), 245–86.

43 Foster, *Age of Agade*, 245–6.

44 Foster, *Age of Agade*, 265–70.

45 Foster, *Age of Agade*, 252–62.

46 Augusta McMahon, 'The Akkadian Period: Empire, Environment, and Imagination', in *A Companion to the Archaeology of the Ancient Near East*, ed. by Daniel T. Potts (Malden, MA: Blackwell Publishing Ltd., 2012), 649–67.

Introduction 13

47 Joan Oates, 'Archaeology in Mesopotamia: Digging Deeper at Tell Brak', *Proc. Br. Ac.* 131 (2005) 1–39, 7, 10; Jean M. Evans, 'Tell Brak in the Akkadian Period', in *Art of the First Cities*, ed. by Joan Aruz and Ronald Wallenfels (New York: Metropolitan Museum of Art, 2003), 228–33; McMahon, 'The Akkadian Period', 654.

48 Zainab Bahrani, *Mesopotamian Ancient Art and Architecture* (London: Thames and Hudson Ltd., 2017), 128.

49 McMahon, 'The Akkadian Period', 655. Francesca de Lillis Forrest, Lucio Milano and Lucia Mori, 'The Akkadian Occupation in the Northwest Area of the Tell Leilan Acropolis', *KASKAL* 4 (2007): 43–64, 46–7.

50 Giorgio Buccellati and Marilyn Kelly-Buccellati, 'The Palace at Urkesh and the Daughter of Naram-Sin', *AAAS* XLIV (2001): 63–70.

51 Giorgio Buccellati and Marilyn Kelly-Buccellati, 'The Great Temple Terrace at Urkesh and the Lions of Tish-atal', in *General Studies and Excavation at Nuzi 11/2 in Honor of David I. Owen on the Occasion of his 65th Birthday October 28, 2005*, ed. by Gernot Wilhelm (Bethesda, MD: CDL Press, 2009), 33–69.

52 Schrakamp, 'A View from Within', 617.

53 Bahrani, *Art and Architecture*, 128–9.

54 Lise A. Truex, 'Households and Institutions: A Late 3rd Millennium BCE Neighborhood at Tell Asmar, Iraq (Ancient Eshnunna)', *AP3A* 30, no. 1 (2019): 39–61, 43.

55 E.g., McMahon, 'The Akkadian Period', 654.

56 McGuire Gibson and Augusta McMahon, 'Investigation of the Early Dynastic-Akkadian Transition: Report on the 18th and 19th Seasons of Excavation in Area WF, Nippur', *Iraq* 57 (1995): 1–39, 9–10.

57 Foster, *Age of Agade*, 188–205.

58 Bahrani, *Art and Architecture*, 113.

59 Foster, *Age of Agade*, 202–5; Irene J. Winter, 'Sex, Rhetoric, and the Public Monument: The Alluring Body of Naram-Sin of Agade', in *Sexuality in Ancient Art: Near East, Egypt, Greece, and Italy*, ed. by Nathalie R. Kampen and Bettina Bergmann (Cambridge: Cambridge University Press, 1996), 11–26.

60 Foster, *Age of Agade*, 188.

61 Melissa Eppihimer, 'Assembling King and State: The Statues of Manishtushu and the Consolidation of Akkadian Kingship', *AJA* 114, no. 3 (2010): 365–80.

62 Bahrani, *Art and Architecture*, 115.

63 Bahrani, *Art and Architecture*, 113.

64 Bahrani, *Art and Architecture*, 119.

65 Friedrich Begermann et al., 'Lead Isotope and Chemical Signature of Copper from Oman and its Occurrence in Mesopotamia and Sites of the Arabian Gulf Coast', *AAE* 21, no. 2 (2010): 135–69.

66 Dominique Collon, *First Impressions. Cylinder Seals in the Ancient Near East* (London: The British Museum Press, 2005), 32.

67 Collon, *First Impressions*, 34.

68 Tatiana Hollier is working on a speculative biography of Enheduana, for instance (https://tatianahollier.com/).

69 Klaus Wagensonner, 'Between History and Fiction – Enheduana, the First Poet in World Literature', in *Women at the Dawn of History*, ed. by Agnete W. Lassen and Klaus Wagensonner (New Haven, CT: Yale University Press, 2020), 38–45; Annette Zgoll, 'Innana and En-hedu-ana: Mutual Empowerment and the Myth INNANA CONQUERS UR', in *Powerful Women in the Ancient World: Perception and (Self) Presentation*, ed. by Kerstin Droß-Krüpe and Sebastian Fink (Zaphon: Münster, 2021), 13–56; Jean-Jacques Glassner, 'En-hedu-ana, une femme auteure en pays de Sumer au IIIe millénaire?' *Topoi: Orient-Occident* 10, no. 1 (2019): 219–31.

14 *Enheduana*

70 E.g., Sophus Helle, 'The Birth of the Author: Co-Creating Authorship in Enheduana's *Exaltation*', *Orb. Litt.* 75, no. 2 (2020): 55–72.

71 It is worth noting, however, Jacob J. Finkelstein's argument that the term means, "land between the river," specifically the bend of the Euphrates River ('Mesopotamia', *Journal of Near Eastern Studies* 21 no. 2 (1962): 73–92, 79).

72 Jerrold S. Cooper, 'Babylonian Beginnings: The Origins of the Cuneiform Writing System in a Comparative Perspective', in *The First Writing: Script Invention as History and Process*, ed. by Stephen Houston (Cambridge: Cambridge University Press, 2006), 71–99.

73 Following Foster, *Age of Agade*, 30–1.

2 The Sargonic Period
History and Legacy

The Historical Context

The Sargonic period was a momentous time in Mesopotamian history. Although it lasted for less than 150 years, it saw profound changes under the impetus of the family who governed Mesopotamia from their capital, Agade. So transformative was this time that the deeds of its rulers, Sargon and Naram-Sin, were immortalized in Sumerian, Akkadian, and Hittite stories for the next 2,000 years.[1] The Sargonic kings were also the first rulers to be incorporated into the Mesopotamian omen tradition, further attesting to their significance in Mesopotamian cultural and historical memory.[2]

This is not to deny the contributions of others, for example, the administrative officials who enacted new practices, and the regional powers and local populations who acted and reacted to the Sargonic rulers' military ambitions. Their undertakings, however, are not as well documented as those of their overlords, so we're left with names and hints of activities, but not many details.

Reconstructing the history of the Sargonic period is challenging, as we rely primarily on royal inscriptions. Although these mention building, repairing, and supporting temples, the Sargonic kings privileged recounting their military successes above all else. One gets the impression that warfare dominated the decades of their rule. This is not inaccurate. Nevertheless, innovation was a hallmark of the Sargonic period, and it affected all areas of life—technology, agriculture, administration, culture, politics, and religion.

The Sargonic period is traditionally dated 2316–2173 BCE, specifically from the time Sargon, the dynastic founder, might have become ruler of Agade, to the death of Shar-kali-sharri, Naram-Sin's son and successor.[3] This was followed by three years of internal confusion, after which two kings claimed the rulership of Agade: Dudu (r. c. 2169–2149 BCE) and his son Shuturul (r. c. 2148–2134 BCE). They do not seem to have had any relation with Sargon's family and typically are not included in the dynasty.[4]

The Sargonic period needs to be understood within the broader context of Mesopotamian history, specifically what happened in the preceding centuries and, to a lesser extent, what transpired after the dynasty's end. During the Early Dynastic period, southern Mesopotamia was politically fragmented

DOI: 10.4324/9781032641164-2

16 *Enheduana*

into a constellation of independent city-states, sometimes vying for access to resources. The names of many survive, but we are best informed about Uruk, Ur, Umma (mod. Tell Jokha), Girsu, Shuruppak (mod. Tell Fara), and Abu Salabikh (ancient name unknown). In the northern part of southern Mesopotamia, a major role was played by Kish (mod. Tell Ingharra), possibly the seat of a powerful local state.[5] In northern Mesopotamia, several polities controlled vast swaths of land. These include the city of Ebla (mod. Tell Mardikh) in northern Syria, Nagar and Urkesh in the Balikh River Basin, and Mari (mod. Tell Hariri) on the west bank of the Euphrates, just north of the modern boundary between Syria and Iraq.

For most of the third millennium BCE, Kish played a major role in the economic, political, and social history of the region. By 2500 BCE, it was the largest city in the known world and had close contacts with the northern kingdoms and the southern city-states.[6] During this time, much of southern Mesopotamia might have been involved in small-scale border disputes, such as the multi-generational conflict between Umma and Lagash (mod. Al-Hiba) for control of the Gu'edena, a portion of land.[7] By the end of the Early Dynastic period, however, Kish had lost its primacy, and at least two southern leaders attempted to gain control of the Mesopotamian alluvium: Enshakushana of Uruk and Lugalzagesi of Umma. This was a significant change in southern politics, as for centuries rulers had limited local power. Although absolute dates are hard to come by, Enshakushana, Lugalzagesi, and Sargon were roughly contemporary at the end of the twenty-fourth century BCE.[8]

Enshakushana was the last ruler of Uruk before Lugalzagesi's conquest. Unlike many of his predecessors and contemporaries, Enshakushana had the resources to expand his control beyond Uruk and its hinterland. Three of Enshakushana's year names commemorate military endeavors against Kish (a siege), Agade (a defeat), and Irisagrig (the seizing of its temple administrator).[9] According to the royal inscriptions of IriKAgina, ruler of Lagash, who was Enshakushana's peer, a man of Uruk (who must be Enshakushana) laid siege to Lagash at least three times.[10] If we are to believe one of his own royal inscriptions, Enshakushana also campaigned successfully against Akshak (modern location unknown) and captured the king of Kish, Enbi-Ishtar.[11]

Presumably emboldened by his conquests, Enshakushana proclaimed himself **en ki-en-gi lugal kalam-ma**, "lord of Sumer, king of the land."[12] Thus, already before Sargon, Mesopotamian rulers had regional, if not transregional, territorial ambitions.[13] Dating Enshakushana's reign, not to mention his military deeds, is currently impossible. It has been suggested that he launched his attacks against IriKAgina sometime around the latter's fourth to sixth regnal years. This roughly corresponds to the early part of Lugalzagesi's reign and precedes Sargon's conquest of southern Mesopotamia by about two decades.[14]

While it is unlikely that Enshakushana ever fully realized his goals, Lugalzagesi of Umma (r. c. 2315–2292 BCE) certainly did. Lugalzagesi's

The Sargonic Period: History and Legacy 17

origins are obscure.[15] He began his career as **ensi**$_2$ ("ruler") of Umma. He succeeded his father Bubu in this position, but the two of them seem not to have belonged to the main branch of the Umma ruling family.[16] Rather, Lugalzagesi might have come from Eresh (location uncertain).[17]

It is unclear how Lugalzagesi grew his territorial control, as evidence is meager. While military actions certainly contributed, one should not disregard the possibility that Lugalzagesi also strengthened his position through political alliances, as the Sargonic and other Mesopotamian rulers did.[18] Crucial was his victory over Uruk, which under Enshakushana had already amassed some territories. The king of Uruk hadn't been fully successful in bringing IriKAgina to bear, a task that Lugalzagesi accomplished. This allowed Lugalzagesi to declare himself king of the land "from the rising of the sun to the setting of the sun."[19] Indeed, one of Lugalzagesi's royal inscriptions states:

> When the god Enlil, king of all the lands, gave to Lugalzagesi the kingship of the land, directed the eyes of the land towards him, put all the lands at his feet, and made them subject to him from east to west; at that time, he (=Enlil) also put the roads in order for him from the Lower Sea along the Tigris and Euphrates to the Upper Sea. From east to west, Enlil allowed no rival for him. Under him (=Lugalzagesi), all foreign lands rested at ease, the (home)land made merry.[20]

As with all Mesopotamian inscriptions, this one, too, is ideologically charged and not entirely reliable. There is no evidence, for instance, that Lugalzagesi ever ventured into modern-day Syria, let alone as far as the Mediterranean (the "Upper Sea" of the document). Nor do we have proof that Lugalzagesi's rule went unchallenged until Sargon came along, as the sentence "Enlil permitted him no rival" implies. Nevertheless, Lugalzagesi represented himself as the ruler of the known world.

It is not a coincidence that the inscription addresses Enlil, a powerful Mesopotamian god who, during the third and early second millennia BCE, was the guarantor of human kingship. He did so from his sanctuary in Nippur, called the Ekur, "House Mountain," where his powerful clergy sanctioned the legitimacy of new rulers.[21] The role bestowed upon Enlil was certainly not Lugalzagesi's innovation. Rather, Enlil had been central to Mesopotamian religious thought in general, and kingship in particular, throughout the third millennium BCE.[22] Thus, Lugalzagesi made a powerful statement: his kingship, which transcended local boundaries, was not ordained by just any deity. It was sanctioned by the king of the gods. The inscription cited above was found on fragments of several stone vessels uncovered at Nippur, likely dedicated to Enlil by Lugalzagesi himself.[23]

Lugalzagesi ruled for at least 25 years, or so the *Sumerian King List* proclaims. This document, however, is as ideologically charged as the royal

18 *Enheduana*

inscriptions.[24] The *Sumerian King List* provides a continuous sequence of rulers organized into dynasties from the time when "kingship descended from heaven" to the last king of the dynasty of Isin (mod. Ishan al-Bahriyat) around 1794 BCE.[25] The historical value of the *Sumerian King List* is limited because it mentions mythical characters with unrealistically long reigns, does not include all dynasties known from contemporary records, and creates a historical fiction wherein only one dynasty ruled Mesopotamia at one time.[26] Yet, it can assist in establishing the approximate length of a king's reign and the order of rulers in a dynasty.[27]

The end of Lugalzagesi's rule came at the hands of Sargon of Agade (r. c. 2316–2277), a king of northern Mesopotamia. Sargon took advantage of the progressive contraction of Kish's power and Enshakushana and Lugalzagesi's successes at centralization to incorporate the Mesopotamian alluvium into his realm.[28] Yet, it would be a mistake to think that there was a significant difference between the last king of the Early Dynastic period and the founder of the Sargonic Dynasty, as Sargon inserted himself into the pre-existing tradition of Early Dynastic rulership.[29]

Indeed, there is a degree of continuity between the Early Dynastic period and the reign of Sargon and his first successor, Rimush—unsurprisingly since this periodization is a modern invention. There is little difference, for instance, between monumental and glyptic art from the reign of Sargon and those of his predecessors.[30] Thus, contest and banquet scenes, which became popular on Early Dynastic seals, continued to be used in the early part of the Sargonic period.

While we are relatively well informed about Sargon's achievements once he conquered the Mesopotamian alluvium, not much is known about his life *before* he began his engagements in the south. Partly, this is because Sargon's capital, Agade, has not yet been identified. Since the core of Sargon's empire was the land of Warium (**Uri**/*Wari'um*), which encompassed the region at the confluence of the Tigris and Adheim Rivers, Agade was most likely situated in this area.[31] The loss of Agade is incommensurable for our understanding of the Sargonic period. With very few exceptions, such as objects raided by Elamites and brought back to Susa, its relics are lost to us.

Nevertheless, much of Agade's monumental artwork was visible centuries after the city was sacked and heavily damaged by enemy armies. Such was the renown of the ancient capital that later rulers felt compelled to repair its old buildings and carry out its traditions. For example, Erridu-pizir (r. c. 2134–2130), a Gutian king who governed over parts of southern Mesopotamia not long after the fall of Agade, performed ritual offerings in Agade.[32]

The devotion of later rulers to the once-Sargonic capital continued in the second millennium and persisted into the mid-first millennium BCE.[33] Nabonidus (r. 556–539 BCE), the last native ruler before the Persian conquest of 539 BCE, was particularly active in Agade.[34] So proud was he for having uncovered the foundations of a temple of Ishtar in Agade (Eulmash) that he commissioned an inscription about it and erected a new foundation and two

The Sargonic Period: History and Legacy 19

ziggurats for Ishtar of Agade.[35] Agade's fame endured, and Mesopotamian rulers participated in its upkeep, thus elevating themselves to the status of kings whose deeds had not been forgotten almost 2,000 years later.

It was from Agade that Sargon ruled. Whether he had been born there is unknown. Indeed, the question of Sargon's origins is as thorny as that of Lugalzagesi's. No contemporary sources elucidate Sargon's birth and early years, or how he became king. And while it is generally agreed that Sargon must have ruled for more than 18 years before he defeated Lugalzagesi around 2292 BCE, what happened before and during these years is unclear.[36]

Later traditions, discussed in the second part of this chapter, name Sargon's father, a man called La'ibum, who does not appear to have held a political office.[37] They also tie Sargon to Kish, where he allegedly was born and grew up, served as the cupbearer of the local ruler, Ur-Zababa, and eventually rebelled against him to create his own kingdom.[38] The *Sumerian King List* agrees with this narrative: "In Agade, Sargon, whose father was a gardener, the cupbearer of Ur-Zababa, became king of Agade, who built Agade (itself)."[39] However, the *Sumerian King List* credits Ur-Zababa with an impossible reign of 400 years.[40] While documents from the northern Syrian city of Ebla mention a king of Kish who some argue was Sargon himself, further confirmation of Sargon's rise to power is not secured in contemporary sources.[41]

It is unlikely that Sargon founded the city of Agade, as the *Sumerian King List* wants us to believe. One of Enshakushana's regnal years was named "The Year when Enshakushana defeated Agade."[42] This commemoration would suggest a lofty achievement, such as the defeat of a famous and long-standing center, rather than the destruction of a newly erected one.

These unresolved questions have implications for Enheduana's early life. She spent most of her adult life in the southern city of Ur, where she was the high priestess of the poliad moon god Nanna/Sin. Her appointment seems to have occurred not long after Sargon's conquest of the south in 2292 BCE. However, she was born and raised elsewhere—whether in Kish, Agade, or another city, is unknown.

Finally, documents disagree about the length of Sargon's reign. Four manuscripts of the *Sumerian King List* preserve different dates: the oldest extant manuscript, which dates to the twenty-first century BCE, counts 40 years. Three manuscripts from the eighteenth century BCE offer 54, 55, and 56 years, respectively.[43] I opted to follow the twenty-first-century tradition and attribute to Sargon 40 regnal years (c. 2316–2276 BCE).[44]

Sargon's accomplishments are typically reconstructed using the numerous royal inscriptions he commissioned, the names of his regnal years, and the administrative documents from his reign. Sargon's conquest of the north likely occurred before he turned his attention to the Mesopotamian alluvium and the kingdom of Lugalzagesi. Thus, Syrian cities such as Ebla and Mari were attacked and destroyed before 2292 BCE.[45] Afterwards, Sargon waged war against Lugalzagesi, defeated him, and proclaimed that:

20   *Enheduana*

Sargon ... conquered the city of Uruk and destroyed its city-walls. He fought against the leader of Uruk and defeated him. He fought with Lugalzagesi, king of Uruk, captured him and took him to the gate of the god Enlil in a neck stock.[46]

This inscription survives only in Old Babylonian copies made by student scribes learning cuneiform.[47] Its original, written in Sumerian and Akkadian, must have been inscribed on steles decorated with martial scenes to illustrate the narrative.[48] These steles were erected in the Ekur, the temple of Enlil at Nippur, where Lugalzagesi and Sargon, too, received legitimization.[49] The city of Nippur continued to have a significant role in the Sargonic ideology of kingship.[50]

Sargon also campaigned extensively outside of Mesopotamia, for example against the eastern polity of Elam, in modern-day western Iran, against **Marhashi**/*Parhashum* in southern Iran, and against Magan.[51] Indeed, the Sargonic drive in Iran was unprecedented, continued throughout the dynasty, and had important cultural and ideological ramifications for Mesopotamian history.[52]

When and how these expeditions occurred is unclear, but the implementation of a standing professional army that used innovative military techniques must have played a significant role in Sargon's success. Worth noting are the introduction of the superior composite bow, as well as "battle tactics based on the use of long-range weapons," although these weapons had already been in use during the Early Dynastic period.[53]

The land under Sargon's control was reorganized, but our documentation for this process comes exclusively from southern Mesopotamia. The extent to which Sargon restructured northern Mesopotamia is currently unknown. Fundamental to Sargon's state control was a systematic centralization process, including the adoption of Sargon's year names in local calendars and the use of the Akkadian *kor* as a unit of measurement.[54] Yet, local administrative practices and, more importantly, local administrators were left in place. This eventually backfired, as it created circumstances for the southern potentates to rebel.

Enheduana herself was instrumental in her father's strategy to secure control over the south. Not long after 2292 BCE, Sargon installed her in one of the most prestigious priestly offices of the land. By doing so, Sargon "certainly infring[ed] upon the privileges of the local elites, who had previously claimed [this] right."[55] It is not surprising that almost 60 years later, when Lugal-Ane rebelled against Naram-Sin, he forcibly removed Enheduana from her seat—at least according to *Inana B*.

We have no information about Sargon's death, not even in the later traditions that recast him as an almost superhuman hero.[56] He was succeeded by two of his sons, Rimush and Manishtushu. The succession order is unclear since the manuscripts of the *Sumerian King List* are not in agreement. The

The Sargonic Period: History and Legacy 21

earliest manuscript lists Manishtushu before Rimush.[57] Manishtushu's own name, "Who is with him?," could arguably point to him being the firstborn, or simply be a rhetorical question—the answer to which is "no one" since he is without rivals.[58] However, later manuscripts of the *Sumerian King List* invert this order, and scholars have followed along by positioning Rimush before Manishtushu.[59] We also know nothing about the Sargonic rules of primogeniture, and so the new king need not have been the firstborn son. Without clear evidence, I opted to follow the most accepted sequence of Rimush/Manishtushu, although a Manishtushu/Rimush sequence is equally possible and would change the reconstruction proposed below.

Rimush ruled 7 (followed here), 9, or 15 years.[60] Upon inheriting his father's throne, Rimush (r. c. 2276–2270 BCE) was confronted with a major rebellion of southern forces; he squashed it so brutally that there wasn't another one for more than 40 years.[61] Not content with having annihilated his enemies, Rimush began to confiscate southern lands, possibly "mark[ing] the beginning of the establishment of royal agricultural domains in the Sumerian south."[62] This had important repercussions for the royal family, who continued to grow its wealth, and for the local families that saw their ancient privileges evaporate. Like Sargon, Rimush, too, campaigned in the east against Elam and Marhashi, thereby demonstrating the tenuous hold that the Sargonic state had on its eastern borders.[63]

Information about Rimush's demise comes from omen texts. These documents were part of the toolkit of the diviner, a Mesopotamian specialist who interpreted natural phenomena to decode messages from the gods. A second-millennium omen reads: "Omen of Rimush, whom his servants killed with their cylinder seals (or: their sealed documents)." The first-millennium text is the same but replaces "servants" with "courtiers."[64]

Given the nature of these texts, and the fact that they were written centuries after Rimush's death, their reliability as historical sources is questionable. This does not negate the possibility that Rimush's death was incorporated into the omen tradition *because* he had been killed in a court conspiracy. If so, a likely culprit might have been his brother Manishtushu, who succeeded him on the throne and whose line survived through his son Naram-Sin and his grandson, Shar-kali-sharri. This is provided, of course, that the *Sumerian King List* is correct in its claim that Naram-Sin was Manishtushu's son, and not Rimush's. Sargonic rulers did not identify their fathers in their royal inscriptions.

Unsurprisingly, the length of Manishtushu's reign is also unclear. According to our sources, he governed for at most 15 years, a number followed widely by scholars and here as well (c. 2269–2254 BCE).[65] Manishtushu continued his brother's policy of land expropriation, as witnessed by his most famous monument, the Obelisk of Manishtushu. It records the sale of a large portion of land (approximately 3,430 hectars) located around the cities of Dur-Sin (modern location unknown), Girtab (modern location unknown),

22   *Enheduana*

Marad (mod. Tell as-Sadoum), and Kish by local families. Yet, one suspects the sellers were not given much choice. The land was most likely redistributed to the witnesses of the transaction, 49 citizens of Agade loyal to the crown.[66] This process must have exacerbated the malcontent among the southern elite, which eventually erupted in the Great Revolt.

Manishtushu's engagements abroad are poorly documented, although he led at least one campaign in the southeast.[67] Likely, the crown had gone in search of new sources of profitable raw materials. One royal inscription refers to "cities across the Sea (...) assembled for battle," which Manishtushu overpowered.[68] Emphasis is placed on the plundering of silver mines and the quarrying of an unidentified black stone.[69]

Royal statuary was a strategic tool in Manishtushu's consolidation of power.[70] Numerous fragments of Manishtushu's diorite, dolerite, or olivine gabbro statues have been unearthed throughout the Near East.[71] Typically, these statues represent Manishtushu standing or seated, and the inscription, as well as the objects themselves, were standardized.[72] Emphasis was placed on naturalism, and attention was devoted to representing the human body accurately. To do so, Manishtushu must have engaged incredibly skilled and innovative sculptors.[73] The choice of material is also noteworthy. Diorite had to be imported from Oman. By using a material that had been "conquered" from a foreign land, Manishtushu's control over the diorite trade represented what he was never able to achieve in practice: hegemony over neighboring lands.

Manishtushu's statues were erected in the temples of major deities at Nippur (Enlil), Uruk (An and Inana/Ishtar, or Ashtar during the Sargonic period), Sippar (mod. Tell Abu Habbah; Utu/Shamash), Ur (Nanna/Sin), and Agade (Ashtar).[74] By doing so, Manishtushu attempted to create a level of equality in his relationships with the most important gods of the pantheon. Indeed, "[r]ather than elevate Akkade and its god (Ishtar) or make himself a god as Naram-Sin would later do, Manishtushu equitably inserted himself into the highest level of authority in each city."[75]

Was Manishtushu successful? It's hard to tell. On the one hand, no rebellions are documented for his reign, possibly an accident of discovery. On the other hand, about 25 years after Manishtushu's death, Naram-Sin had to face the southern cities in the Great Revolt. The reality is that the Sargonic rulers never found an effective way to control the centrifugal forces pushing for a return to the political fragmentation that had been the way of life for centuries before Lugalzagesi's conquest.

Manishtushu, too, was killed in a palace conspiracy, at least if we are to believe the omen tradition. A second millennium text reads: "Omen of Manishtushu, whom his palace (or: ministers?) killed."[76] It is possible, of course, "that Manishtusu's death was confused or conflated with Rimush's assassination."[77] Alternatively, Manishtushu might have been eliminated by Naram-Sin himself. If the latter was Rimush's son, he may have asserted what he believed was his right to the throne.

The Sargonic Period: History and Legacy   23

Naram-Sin's reign (c. 2253–2198 BCE) is the best documented among the Sargonic rulers, but its length is uncertain. The oldest manuscript of the *Sumerian King List* assigns him 54 regnal years, while later tablets are consistent in listing 56.[78] Under Naram-Sin, a series of far-reaching internal reforms and the implementation of a recognizable foreign policy were enacted.[79] The kingdom, which under Naram-Sin reached its maximum expansion, was divided into provinces whose boundaries followed those of past city-states. Provinces situated in the northern part of southern Mesopotamia were controlled directly by the royal family, specifically by the king's sons. For the southern provinces, however, the situation is murkier. Scholars debate whether southern governors were members of local families appointed by the king but able to operate independently or rather fully integrated into the Sargonic system.[80]

One of the most significant events during Naram-Sin's reign was the Great Revolt, which occurred around 2230 BCE.[81] The rebellion of southern provinces led by Iphur-Kish, king of Kish, Amar-girid, king of Uruk, and Lugal-Ane, king of Ur (at least according to the literary tradition) involved numerous cities, such as Kazallu (modern location unknown), Kutha (mod. Tell Ibrahim), and Sippar.[82] In his account of the events, Naram-Sin reports that the city of Agade was attacked on all fronts, but he was able to prevent defeat at every turn:[83]

> Naram-Sin, the mighty, king of Agade, when the four quarters rebelled against him together, was victorious in nine battles in a single year through the love Ishtar bore him and captured the kings whom they had had raised up against him. Because he defended the foundation of his city while in danger, (the people of his) city asked (numerous gods) that he be made god of their city, Agade.[84]

This was a significant break in tradition since no king had ever deified himself. Besides his self-deification, Naram-Sin began using a new title, "king of the four corners (of the universe)," to stress his dominion over the known world.[85]

Not long after Naram-Sin quashed the rebellion, Enheduana, by then an old woman, died of unknown causes.[86] Naram-Sin appointed his own daughter to replace her and commemorated the event in a year name: "[Year] when the high priestess of Nanna, daughter of Naram-Sin, was appointed by oracle."[87] We know the name she took once she became high priestess from two inscriptions uncovered at Ur. While one contains only her name on a door socket, the other (in Akkadian on a clay tablet) is longer:[88]

> [Naram-Sin, king of the] f[our quarters]: Enmena[na], *zirru* of Nanna, spouse of Nanna, high priestess of the god Sin at Ur (is) his daughter.

24 *Enheduana*

For how long Enmenana ("The high priestess is the crown of the sky/An") held the office is unknown. The next documented high priestess of Nanna/Sin at Ur was Enanepada ("The high priestess chosen by An"), daughter of Ur-Bau of Lagash, who ruled an independent city in the mid-twenty-second century BCE, after Shar-kali-sharri's death.[89]

Naram-Sin's campaigns abroad are well documented, although their chronology is unclear. He engaged in the north and the west, going as far as the Cedar Forest, presumably located in the Amanus Mountains, in modern-day Lebanon. He launched attacks against Elam, Marhashi, and Magan, trying to secure lands that his predecessors had failed to control. Sargonic presence during the reign of Naram-Sin is also well documented in northern Mesopotamia, where both Nagar and Gasur were seats of imperial power.[90] Naram-Sin relied on diplomacy, too—for example, one of his daughters, Taram-Agade, was married to the king of Urkesh.[91]

Naram-Sin is remembered not only as a successful military leader but also as a great builder and reformer. He sponsored the construction of numerous temples across the realm, including, presumably, the one in his own honor at Agade. During his reign, and most likely under the initiative of his officials, a series of ameliorations were introduced to facilitate the running of the land. Among others, the central administration reformed record-keeping and writing practices, implemented changes in sealing practices, and introduced a standardized system of weights and measures.[92] Additionally, classical Sargonic Akkadian became widespread as the language of the administration, although this might be the culmination of a process rather than Naram-Sin's own innovation.[93]

Finally, trends in artistic production begun under Manishtushu found full realization during Naram-Sin's long reign. The *Victory Stele of Naram-Sin* (Figure 2.1) attests to the achievements of Sargonic artists. It displays the king victorious over enemy soldiers with extraordinary naturalism and an emphasis on the masculinity of the king's body. Naram-Sin is represented wearing a single-horned cap, stressing his divinity and previously worn only by deities.[94] Moreover, artists depicted the landscape, albeit in a stylized manner, indicating the king's control of the people *and* the land.

Glyptic art also changed during the reigns of Naram-Sin (and Shar-kali-sharri), as artists introduced a new repertoire of images. Two typologies are worth mentioning: mythological scenes, and the representation of the sun god, Utu (Sumerian)/Shamash (Akkadian).[95] The popularity of the sun god on seals was connected with the fact that, in the Semitic world, he was not just the god of the sun but also the god of justice on earth and, presumably, in the netherworld.[96] Hence, he was a comforting figure who brought order and balance to the living and the dead.

Since no Sargonic literature survives outside of school texts, the mythological scenes depicted on seals represent one of the few windows we have into the Sargonic conceptualization of the cosmos and the supernatural beings

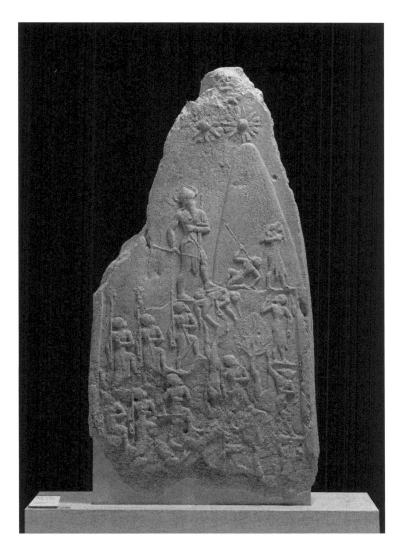

Figure 2.1 Victory Stele of Naram-Sin, Sargonic Period. From Susa. Courtesy of the Musée du Louvre.

26 *Enheduana*

that inhabited it. Indeed, it is from the glyptic evidence that we know about the essential roles the three astral deities Shamash (the sun), Sin (the moon), and Ashtar (the planet Venus) played in the Akkadian pantheon.[97]

Although a deified king who left behind quite a legacy, Naram-Sin still died a man, albeit not a young one. The circumstances of his death are unknown; even the omen tradition is silent on the matter. His son, Shar-kali-sharri (r. c. 2197–2173 BCE), inherited his throne, but he had already been active during Naram-Sin's reign, having campaigned with him as the crown prince.[98] Shar-kali-sharri ruled for about 25 years over an increasingly weakened kingdom.[99] His royal titles were more modest than his predecessors', and his military campaigns had a defensive scope.[100] The chronology of events is unclear, so we do not know when various regions began to break away. Only one son is attested for Shar-kali-sharri; his name was Sharatigubisin, and he did not become king.[101] According to later omen traditions, Shar-kali-sharri, too, was killed by his servants. His name was later associated with the fall of Agade, although not to the extent that his father's was.[102] After Shar-kali-sharri's death, the land reverted to the political fragmentation typical of the Early Dynastic period.

The Sargonic rulers were constantly on the warpath, even when matters were quiet at home—at least this is the impression their inscriptions convey. Interdynastic marriages and commercial contacts also played a role in international relations. Trade with Susa, Dilmun (modern-day Bahrain), Magan, and Meluhha (Indus River Valley) is particularly well documented.[103] Akkadian texts uncovered at Susa indicate it held a central role in the international trade network that the Sargonic rulers and their merchants established.[104] The movement of goods, including semi-precious and precious stones, building materials, and metals, enriched the coffers of the crown and facilitated Sargonic building programs, military expeditions, and the general prosperity of the ruling class.

The causes for the fall of the Sargonic state have been the topic of much debate.[105] Internal centrifugal forces—combined with possible small and/or large-scale climate changes—as well as external pressure from neighboring regions were contributing factors. The *Sumerian King List* informs us that, after three years of unrest, Dudu and Shuturul, who never claimed relation with the Sargonic rulers, governed for a combined approximately 25 years.[106] Their territorial possessions were vastly smaller than their predecessors'.[107] Thereafter, Agade came under the control a the Gutian ruler, Erridu-pizir.[108]

After a few decades of political disintegration, wherein local dynasties flourished once again, the land was centralized under the Third Dynasty of Ur (c. 2112–2004 BCE). From this moment forward, the exceptional achievements of Sargon and Naram-Sin were immortalized in the historiographical tradition.

The Memory of the Kings of Agade

While all Sargonic rulers were remembered in later omen traditions, only Sargon and Naram-Sin became the protagonists of legends.[109] Compositions about them were written mostly in Akkadian several centuries after the fall of Agade. The *Sumerian Sargon Legend* (also known as *Sargon and Ur-Zababa*) and the *Curse of Agade*, however, were written in Sumerian.

The *Sumerian Sargon Legend* survives on two Old Babylonian manuscripts, and it likely originated in the cultural milieu of the Third Dynasty of Ur. The composition speaks of Sargon's early years: he was born to La'ibum, whose profession is not mentioned, and a woman whose name is lost in a break. Sargon rose to prominence in the court of Ur-Zababa of Kish, becoming the king's cupbearer under Inana's protection. In the tradition of heroes the world around, Sargon had a prophetic dream: he saw Inana drowning Ur-Zababa in a river of blood and, concerned for his king, shared the dream with him. Ur-Zababa understood the dream for what it was: a warning that Sargon would overthrow him and rule in his stead. He enlisted the assistance of Lugalzagesi, king of Uruk, to eliminate Sargon. Unfortunately, the rest of the story is lost, but it is not hard to imagine Sargon emerging victorious.[110]

The veracity of the *Sumerian Sargon Legend* is impossible to determine. Sargon and Lugalzagesi are historical figures reimagined in a coming-of-age tale. Ur-Zababa is likely not; his 400-year-long reign (per the *Sumerian King List*) and the lack of inscriptions in his name speak to this. Yet, the story does not describe unrealistic events. Sargon might have begun his career as an official at the Kishite court. He did wage war against Lugalzagesi, although likely not at another king's instigation. Thus, this account, like all those about Sargon and Naram-Sin, carefully treads the line between history and fiction.

The *Curse of Agade* was written within 60 years of the fall of the Sargonic empire, and it survives in twenty-first- and eighteenth-century manuscripts.[111] It attributes the dynasty's demise to the impiety of Naram-Sin, whose reconstruction of the temple of Enlil at Nippur is recast as a sacrilegious act.[112] According to the composition, Naram-Sin attacked *and* demolished the temple in retaliation for having received omens against erecting a temple to his own poliad deity, Inana.[113] Enraged by Naram-Sin's actions, Enlil commanded that the Gutians invade and wreak havoc in Mesopotamia. During this attack, Agade was destroyed.

Why Naram-Sin was cast in such a terrible light is difficult to pinpoint. On the one hand, the *Curse of Agade* belongs to the genre of city laments, which highlight the devastation that divine powers could cause among humankind.[114] A subset of lamentations, city laments mostly date to the late third and early second millennia BCE, and the *Curse of Agade* is the earliest attested. On the other hand, the *Curse of Agade* is unique because it puts the responsibility for the destruction of Agade firmly in the hands of its king, a historical figure.

28 *Enheduana*

Moreover, it was written not long after the end of the Sargonic Dynasty, when the memory of events must still have been vivid.

Why, then, did the authors attribute the collapse of Naram-Sin's empire to his impiety? It was historically inaccurate, and these authors, most likely scholars serving the rulers of Ur, must have been aware of this, if for no other reason than that Agade was still standing. Similarly, as demonstrated by the *Sumerian King List*, which existed within the same scholarly milieu, the authors must have known that the last king of the dynasty was Shar-kali-sharri, not Naram-Sin. Possibly, the Ur elite, whose immediate ancestors had suffered greatly at the hands of Naram-Sin during the Great Revolt, might have played a role in rewriting Sargonic history and casting Naram-Sin as the villain of the story—and of history. From being a ruler who deployed the written word to his own advantage, Naram-Sin was transformed through that same means into a victim of his own ambitions.

While only two Sumerian tales about the rulers of Agade survive, more are preserved in Akkadian. Written during the second and first millennia BCE, these texts "reflect the contradictory judgments of Babylonian thought, according to which striving against impossible odds made one either the hero or the fool."[115] Thus, they echo motifs already present in the *Sumerian Sargon Legend* and the *Curse of Agade*.

At least seven compositions focus on Sargon.[116] Among them, the *Sargon Birth Legend*, preserved on three tablets from the seventh century BCE, portrays Sargon as a precursor of Moses, Cyrus of Persia, and Romulus and Remus: an infant of unknown origins who became a leader among his people. The opening of the composition reads:

> Sargon, the mighty king, king of Akkade, am I. My mother was a high priestess(?), my father I never knew. My father's brother inhabits the highlands. My city is Azupirānu, which lies on the bank of the Euphrates. She conceived me, my high priestess mother, in concealment she gave me birth. She set me in a wicker basket, with bitumen she made my opening water-tight. She cast me down into the river from which I could not ascend. The river bore me, to Aqqi the water-drawer it brought me.[117]

Thereafter, Sargon's rise to power is attributed to the love Ishtar held for him, similarly to how the *Sumerian Sargon Legend* attributed his successes to Inana's love. A list of his achievements follows, after which the story is poorly preserved. Seemingly, Sargon challenged his successors to rule as well as he did.[118]

Like the *Sumerian Sargon Legend*, this composition recasts Sargon as a hero. Describing his mother as a high priestess might be connected to the role this office played in Sargon's consolidation of power in southern Mesopotamia through his own daughter Enheduana. Not much is known about Sargon's father, as we've seen, except for his name. As for Azupiranu, no city bearing

The Sargonic Period: History and Legacy   29

this name is attested, although, "its meaning, 'a specific *azupīru*-like spice and medicinal plant,' is well known."[119] Most Akkadian Sargon legends focus on his deeds, as in *The King of Battle* and *Sargon, the Conquering Hero*.[120] The popularity that some of them had among the Hittites, an Indo-European people who ruled over Anatolia (modern-day Türkiye) for approximately 400 years (c. 1600–1200 BCE), is noteworthy. The Hittite elite who consumed these texts must have had antiquarian interests. Moreover, the framework provided by the Sargonic rulers transcended the regional and cultural differences between Mesopotamia and its neighbors. They provided paradigmatic examples of kingship also to the Hittites—Sargon, the successful campaigner, and Naram-Sin, the impious king.[121]

As for Naram-Sin, five Akkadian compositions survive, and they focus on two events: the Great Revolt and his siege of Apishal.[122] While the historicity of the Great Revolt is confirmed by Naram-Sin's royal inscriptions, nothing is known about the king's alleged involvement with Apishal.[123] The siege is documented elsewhere only in the omen tradition. This does not preclude the possibility that Naram-Sin campaigned against Apishal, which might have been located not far from Alalakh (mod. Tell Atchana), in northern Syria.[124]

Besides the Sumerian *Curse of Agade*, the most popular story about Naram-Sin was the *Cuthean Legend* (or *Naram-Sin and the Enemy Hordes*), originally composed during the early second millennium BCE, but copied well into the first millennium BCE.[125] It portrays Naram-Sin's reckoning with the consequences of his own poor decisions. Specifically, since he did not follow the divine will, Naram-Sin "must realize and acknowledge his tragic error before he can receive assistance from the gods."[126] The occasion for such a sacrilege was Naram-Sin's dismissal of an oracular message about how to deal with the Umman-manda, the enemy hordes. The status quo was ultimately re-established with a clear message: it was the ruler's responsibility to leave instructions for his successors on how to deal with a problem, thus preventing them from being as helpless as Naram-Sin had been.

Naram-Sin's negative depiction in the *Cuthean Legend* echoes motifs introduced by the *Curse of Agade*. Indeed, "[w]hile Sargon's fame in later times was almost wholly favorable, Naramsin's was mixed."[127] When, where, and why such a dichotomy developed is difficult to ascertain. Even if no rebellions are attested for the reign of Sargon, he must have been unpopular among his conquered subjects. Yet, he was spared the harsher criticism his grandson endured.

Besides the omen and literary traditions, the kings of Agade were remembered in historical chronicles such as the late second millennium BCE *Chronicle of the Esagila*, which draws on earlier materials, now lost.[128] Its focus is the worship of the Babylonian god Marduk, and how past rulers showed their devotion to him and his temple, the Esagila.[129] When it comes to the section on the Akkadian rulers, the document is anachronistic since the

30 *Enheduana*

cult of Marduk did not rise in popularity until the second millennium BCE. Yet, the chronicle, too, depicts Sargon in a favorable light, and Naram-Sin in a negative one, directly attributing to him the fall of Agade.[130] Such a dichotomy between the two rulers therefore transcended literary genres.

This was the world in which Enheduana lived. This was what her family members chose to commemorate, and what subsequent generations of scholars opted to preserve, study, elaborate upon, and re-invent. Incidentally, like her father and her grandnephew, Enheduana, too, became associated with noteworthy but at times non-historical endeavors, although hers were of the literary kind. Later scribes re-imagined her accomplishments as they did with her father's and her grandnephew's. We will address this, and other matters, in the ensuing chapters.

Notes

1 Westenholz, *Legends*, 1–3.
2 Foster, *Age of Agade*, 252.
3 Following the dates used in Schrakamp, 'A View from Within', 612–85.
4 While Dudu was certainly king of Agade, as seal inscriptions of his officials attest, his origins are unclear. He never claimed descent from Shar-kali-sharri. Shuturul was Dudu's son. Sallaberger and Schrakamp, *History and Philology*, 110–2, label this phase the Late Akkad period.
5 Dorota Lawecka, 'Early Dynastic Kish: City State or Country-State?' in *Proceedings of the 8th International Congress on the Archeology of the Ancient Near East*, ed. by Piotr Bieliński et al. (Wiesbaden: Harrassowitz Verlag, 2014), 425–39.
6 Norman Yoffee, 'Towards a Biography of Kish: Notes on Urbanism and Comparison', in *Literature as Politics, Politics as Literature: Essays on the Ancient Near East in Honor of Peter Machinist*, ed. by David S. Vanderhooft and Abraham Winitzer (Cambridge: McDonald Institute for Archaeological Research, 2013), 527–44, 529–33.
7 Jerrold S. Cooper, *Reconstructing History from Ancient Inscriptions: The Lagash-Umma Border Conflict* (Malibu, CA: Undena Press, 1983). For a different view on Early Dynastic conflicts, see Seth Richardson, 'Early Mesopotamia: The Presumptive State', *Past & Present* 215 (2012): 3–49, 10–5.
8 Sallaberger and Schrakamp, *History and Philology*, 86–7, 90, and Table 21.
9 Sallaberger and Schrakamp, *History and Philology*, 41. The location of Irisagrig is uncertain.
10 Sallaberger and Schrakamp, *History and Philology*, 85–6.
11 RIME 1.14.17.1.
12 RIME 1.14.17.1, ll. 4–5.
13 Nshan Thomas Kesecker, 'Lugalzagesi: the First Emperor of Mesopotamia?' *AJNES* XII, no. 1 (2018): 76–95, 81.
14 Sallaberger and Schrakamp, *History and Philology*, 85–90 and Table 21.
15 But see Piotr Steinkeller, 'The Question of Lugalzagesi's Origins', in *Festschrift für Burkhart Kienast zu seinem 70. Geburtstage dargebracht von Freunden, Schülern und Kollegen*, ed. by Gebhard J. Selz (Münster: Ugarit-Verlag, 2003), 621–37.
16 Kesecker, 'Lugalzagesi', 80

The Sargonic Period: History and Legacy 31

17 Piotr Michalowski, 'The Kingdom of Akkad in Contact with the World', in *The Oxford History of the Ancient Near East: Volume I: From the Beginning to Old Kingdom Egypt and the Dynasty of Akkad*, ed. by Karen Radner, Nadine Moeller and Daniel T. Potts (Oxford: Oxford University Press, 2020), 686–764, 705.

18 Kesecker, 'Lugalzagesi', 82–4.

19 Kesecker, 'Lugalzagesi', 76–95.

20 RIME 1.14.20.1 col. i ll. 36–46, col. ii ll. 1–20.

21 Jacob Klein, Marten Stol and Marten P. Streck, 'Nippur. A', *RlA* 9 (1998–2001): 532–46; McGuire Gibson, Donald P. Hansen and Richard L. Zettler, 'Nippur B. Archäologisch.', *RlA* 9 (1998–2001): 546–65; Wilfred G. Lambert, 'Nippur in Ancient Ideology', in *Nippur at the Centennial*, ed. by Maria deJong Ellis (Philadelphia, PA: The University Museum, 1992), 119–26.

22 Gebhard J. Selz, 'Enlil und Nippur nach Präsargonischen Quellen', in *Nippur at the Centennial*, ed. by Maria deJong Ellis (Philadelphia, PA: The University Museum, 1992), 189–225; Piotr Michalowski, 'The Unbearable Lightness of Enlil', in *Intellectual Life of the Ancient Near East: Papers Presented at the 43rd Rencontre assyriologique internationale, Prague, July 1–5, 1996*, ed. by Jiri Prosecky (Prague: Academy of Sciences of the Czech Republic, Oriental Institute, 1998), 237–47.

23 Douglas R. Frayne, *Presargonic Period. Early Periods, Volume 1 (2700–2350 BC)* (Toronto/Buffalo/New York: The University of Toronto Press, 2008), 434.

24 Gianni Marchesi, 'The Sumerian King List and the Early History of Mesopotamia', in *ana turri gimilli. Studi dedicati al Padre Werner R. Mayer, S.J. da amici e allievi*, ed. by Maria Giovanna Biga and Mario Liverani (Rome: Dipartimento di Scienze Storiche, Archeologiche e Antropologiche dell'Antichità, Sezione Vicino Oriente, 2010), 231–48.

25 *Sumerian King List*, l. 1

26 Piotr Michalowski, 'History as Charter: Some Observations on the Sumerian King List', *JAOS* 103 (1983): 237–48.

27 The *Sumerian King List* might have been composed during the Sargonic period (Marchesi, 'Sumerian King List', 233). Its earliest extant manuscript dates to the Third Dynasty of Ur (Piotr Steinkeller, 'An Ur III Manuscript of the Sumerian King List', in *Literatur, Politik und Recht in Mesopotamien. Festschrift für Claus Wilcke*, ed. by Walther Sallaberger, Konrad Volk, and Annette Zgoll [Wiesbaden: Harrassowitz Verlag, 2003], 267–92).

28 Michalowski, 'The Kingdom of Akkad in Contact with the World', 702–3.

29 McMahon, 'The Akkadian Period', 650.

30 Collon, *First Impressions*, 32.

31 Agade was most likely situated near the confluence of the Adhem (Adheim, Uzaym) and Tigris Rivers, in proximity to modern Samarra. See Schrakamp, 'A View from Within', 612–4.

32 RIME 2.2.1.2 col. v, ll. 12–18; Eppihimer, *Exemplars of Kingship*, 56.

33 Susanne Paulus, 'Akkade in mittelbabylonischer Zeit', in *Entre les fleuves–II. D'Aššur a Mari et au-delà*, ed. by Nele Ziegler and Eva Cancik-Kirschbaum (Gladbeck: PeWe Verlag, 2014), 199–206.

34 Irene J. Winter, 'Babylonian Archaeologists of the(ir) Mesopotamian Past', in *On the Art of the Ancient Near East Volume II: From the Third Millennium BCE*, by Irene J. Winter (Leiden/Boston: Brill, 2010), 461–80.

35 BM 104738 col ii. ll. 28–78, excerpts; translation after Grant Frame, 'Nabonidus and the History of the Eulmaš Temple at Akkad', *Mesopotamia* XXVIII (1993): 21–50, 24–5.

36 Sallaberger and Schrakamp, *History and Philology*, 93.

32 *Enheduana*

37 The name is preserved in the *Sumerian Sargon Legend*, l. 11. Jerrold S. Cooper and Wolfgang Heimpel, 'The Sumerian Sargon Legend', *JAOS* 103 (1983): 67–82.

38 Westenholz, *Legends*, 51–5.

39 *Sumerian King List*, ll. 266–70.

40 *Sumerian King List*, ll. 247–9.

41 Sallaberger and Schrakamp, *History and Philology*, 90–104; Michalowski, 'The Kingdom of Akkad in Contact with the World', 704.

42 Sallaberger and Schrakamp, *History and Philology*, 41.

43 Sallaberger and Schrakamp, *History and Philology*, 93.

44 Sallaberger and Schrakamp, *History and Philology*, 90–104. Foster, *Age of Agade*, 6, prefers 56 years.

45 Sallaberger and Schrakamp, *History and Philology*, 100 and 105.

46 RIME 2.1.1.1 ll. 1, 12–29.

47 RIME 2.1.1.1 and RIME 2.1.1.2.

48 This is confirmed by the so-called Stele of Sargon, currently housed at the Louvre, which preserves such imagery but no inscription due to its poor state of preservation (see figure 4.8 on p. 58). See Lorenzo Nigro, 'The Two Steles of Sargon: Iconology and Visual Propaganda at the Beginning of Royal Akkadian Relief', *Iraq* 60 (1998): 85–102, 85–93.

49 Frayne, *Sargonic and Gutian Periods*, 9. The concept of legitimacy as applied to ancient Near Eastern rulers has recently been challenged by Seth Richardson, 'Down with "Legitimacy": On "Validity" and Narrative in Royal Tales', in *Tales of Royalty. Notions of Kingship in Visual and Textual Narratives in the Ancient Near East*, ed. by Elisabeth Wagner-Durand and Julia Linke (Berlin: De Gruyter, 2020), 243–60.

50 Schrakamp, 'A View from Within', 652. Particularly informative in this regard is the so-called Onion Archive from Nippur, for which see Aage Westenholz, *Old Sumerian and Old Akkadian Texts in Philadelphia, Part 2: the "Akkadian" Texts, the Enlilmeba Texts and the Onion Archive* (Copenhagen: Museum Tusculanum Press, 1987).

51 Michalowski, 'The Kingdom of Akkad in Contact with the World', 701–14.

52 The influx of foreign goods impacted Sargonic culture in different ways, including textiles and clothing, as discussed by Benjamin R. Foster, 'Clothing in Sargonic Mesopotamia', in *Textile Terminologies in the Ancient Near East and Mediterranean from the Third to the First Millennia BC*, ed. by Cécile Michel and Marie-Louise Nosch (Oxford and Oakville: Oxbow Books, Limited, 2010), 110–45. Indeed, Foster argues that a toga-like garment that became fashionable among the elite during the reign of Manishtushu might find its origins in Manishtushu's own encounters with the clothing he saw in the east (Foster, 'Clothing', 132).

53 Schrakamp, 'A View from Within', 621.

54 Schrakamp, 'A View from Within', 625.

55 Schrakamp, 'A View from Within', 623.

56 Foster, *Age of Agade*, 4, suggests natural causes.

57 Steinkeller, 'An Ur III Manuscript of the Sumerian King List', 272, 278–9.

58 Piotr Steinkeller, 'Man-ištūšu', *RlA* 7 (1987–1990): 334–5, 334.

59 Schrakamp, 'A View from Within', 627.

60 *Sumerian King List*, l. 273; Walter Sommerfeld, 'Rīmuš', *RlA* 11 (2006–8): 372–5.

61 Schrakamp, 'A View from Within', 627; RIME 2.1.2.1.

62 Schrakamp, 'A View from Within', 629; Foster, *The Age of Agade*, 7–8.

63 RIME 2.1.2.6.

64 Foster, *The Age of Agade*, 255.

65 The *Sumerian King List*, l. 277, offers two variants: 7 and 15 years.

The Sargonic Period: History and Legacy 33

66 Steinkeller, 'Man-ištūšu', 335. These lands were granted to fathers and sons, thereby ensuring multi-generational support (Schrakamp, 'A View from Within', 632).

67 Michalowski, 'The Kingdom of Akkad in Contact with the World', 716; Westenholz, 'The Old Akkadian Period', 46.

68 RIME 2.1.3.1, ll. 14–8.

69 RIME 2.1.3.1, ll. 25–30.

70 Eppihimer, 'Assembling King and State', 365–80.

71 Foster, *Age of Agade*, 189.

72 Eppihimer, 'Assembling King and State', 372–5.

73 Foster, *Art of Agade*, 189.

74 Eppihimer, 'Assembling King and State', 376.

75 Eppihimer, 'Assembling King and State', 377.

76 Foster, *Age of Agade*, 255.

77 Foster, *Age of Agade*, 260.

78 *Sumerian King List*, l. 280; Steinkeller, 'An Ur III Manuscript', 272. Following Sallaberger and Schrakamp, *History and Philology*, 108, I opted for 55 years.

79 Michalowski, 'The Kingdom of Akkad in Contact with the World', 723.

80 Schrakamp, 'A View from Within', 632, 634.

81 Schrakamp, 'A View from Within', 632–3; Westenholz, 'The Old Akkadian Period', 51–4; Sallaberger and Schrakamp, *History and Philology*, 108–9.

82 Foster, *Age of Agade*, 12. Naram-Sin mentions only Iphur-Kish and Amar-Girid, but Lugal-Ane's involvement is suggested by the literary tradition.

83 Foster, *Age of Agade*, 12–3. RIME 2.1.4.5.

84 Bassetki Inscription, ll. 1–24, 49–56 = RIME 2.1.4.10.

85 For example, RIME 2.1.4.1, col. ii. ll. 6'–7'; Piotr Michalowski, 'Masters of the Four Corners of the Universe: Views of the Universe in Early Mesopotamian Writing', in *Geography, and Ethnography: Perspective of the World in Pre-Modern Societies*, ed. by Kurt A. Raaflaub and Richard J. A. Talbert (Oxford: Blackwells, 2010), 146–68. This expression can also be translated as "king of the four riverbanks," possibly indicating a new worldview. While earlier Mesopotamian rulers, whose inscriptions were written in Sumerian, emphasized the idea of **kalam**, land, Naram-Sin preferred to draw attention to the two rivers. "[T]he intervening lands were less important in [his] mental maps than the two great rivers and the immediate environs" (anonymous reviewer, personal communication, summer 2024).

86 E.g., Aage Westenholz, 'Assyriologists, Ancient and Modern, on Naramsin and Sharkalisharri', in *Assyriologica et Semitica: Festschrift für Joachim Oelsner*, ed. by J. Marzahn, H. Neumann, and A. Fuchs (Munster: Ugarit-Verlag, 2000), 545–56, 555.

87 Sallaberger and Schrakamp, *History and Philology*, 45.

88 RIME 2.1.4.34 and RIME 2.1.4.33 respectively.

89 For Enanepada see RIME 3/1.1.6.12 and 3/1.1.6.13 in Dietz O. Edzard, *Gudea and His Dynasty* (Toronto/London/Buffalo: The University of Toronto Press, 1997), 24–5.

90 Michalowski, 'The Kingdom of Akkad in Contact with the World', 729–40.

91 Giorgio Buccellati and Marilyn Kelly-Buccellati, 'Tar'am-Agade, Daughter of Naram-Sin, at Urkesh', in *Of Pots and Plans: Papers of the Archeology and History of Mesopotamia and Syria Presented to David Oates*, ed. by Lamia al-Gailani Werr et al. (London: Nabu Publications, 2002), 11–31; Marilyn Kelly-Buccellati, 'Uqnitum and Tar'am-Agade: Patronage and Portraiture at Urkesh', in *Festschrift für Gernot Wilhelm anläßlich seines 65. Geburtstage am 28. Januar 2010*, ed. by Jeannette C. Fincke (Dresden: ISLET Verlag, 2009), 185–202.

34   *Enheduana*

92   Foster, *Age of Agade*, 14–21.
93   Schrakamp, 'A View from Within', 633; Foster, *Age of Agade*, 17–21.
94   Foster, *Age of Agade*, 200.
95   Foster, *Age of Agade*, 203–5. For the role of Shamash during the Sargonic period, see Foster, *The Age of Agade*, 136. For a discussion of the mythological scenes, see Piotr Steinkeller, 'Early Semitic Literature and Third Millennium Seals with Mythological Motifs', *QuadSem* 18 (1993): 243–83.
96   Foster, *Age of Agade*, 205.
97   Foster, *Age of Agade*, 136.
98   Foster, *Age of Agade*, 23.
99   The *Sumerian King List* l. 283 lists 24 or 25 years; Steinkeller, 'An Ur III Manuscript', 272; Sallaberger and Schrakamp, *History and Philology*, 110.
100   Aage Westenholz, 'Šar-kali-šarrī', *RlA* 12 (2009–11): 64–5; Westenholz, 'The Old Akkadian Period', 56–7.
101   Aage Westenholz, 'Šar'atigubisin', *RlA* 12 (2009–11): 35.
102   Foster, *Age of Agade*, 256.
103   Michalowski, 'The Kingdom of Akkad in Contact with the World', 748. Indeed, Sargon was the first Mesopotamian ruler to mention trade in his royal inscriptions.
104   Foster, *Age of Agade*, 180–1; Steffen Laursen and Piotr Steinkeller, *Babylonia, the Gulf Region, and the Indus. Archaeological and Textual Evidence for Contact in the Third and Early Second Millennia BC* (Winona Lake, IN: Eisenbrauns, 2017).
105   Foster, *Age of Agade*, 23–5.
106   *Sumerian King List*, ll. 284–93.
107   Giuseppe Visicato, 'Quello che accade (forse) dopo la morte di Šar-kali-šarri', in *Akkade is King: A Collection of Papers by Friends and Colleagues Presented to Aage Westenholz on the Occasion of his 70th Birthday 15th of May 2009*, ed. by Gojko Barjamovich et al. (Leiden: Nederlands Instituut voor het Nabije Oosten 2011), 227–43, 228–30.
108   Visicato, 'Quello che accade', 230–2.
109   Westenholz, *Legends*; Jerrold S. Cooper, *The Curse of Agade* (Baltimore, MD: The Johns Hopkins University Press, 1983); Mario Liverani, 'Model and Actualization: The Kings of Akkad in the Historical Tradition', in *Akkad: The First World Empire*, ed. by Mario Liverani (Padua: Sargon, 1993), 41–67; Foster, *Age of Agade*, 245–86.
110   Cooper and Heimpel, 'Sumerian Sargon Legend', 76–8.
111   Joan Goodnick Westenholz, 'The Memory of Sargonic Kings Under the Third Dynasty of Ur', in *On the Third Dynasty of Ur: Studies in Honor of Marcel Sigrist*, ed. by Piotr Michalowski (Boston: American School of Oriental Research, 2008), 251–60, 251.
112   Foster, *Age of Agade*, 265–7; Westenholz, 'The Memory of the Sargonic Kings', 252.
113   Cooper, *Curse of Agade*, 5.
114   See e.g., Nili Samet, *The Lamentation over the Destruction of Ur* (Winona Lake, IN: Eisenbrauns, 2014), 1.
115   Foster, *Age of Agade*, 267.
116   Westenholz, *Legends*, 36–49.
117   Translation slightly adapted after Westenholz, *Legends*, 39 and 41.
118   Westenholz, *Legends*, 36.
119   Westenholz, *Legends*, 39.
120   Westenholz, *Legends*, 57–140.
121   Gary Beckman, 'Sargon and Naram-Sin in Hatti: Reflections of Mesopotamian Antiquity among the Hittites', in *Die Gegenwart des Altertums. Formen und*

The Sargonic Period: History and Legacy   35

Funktionen des Altertumsbezugs in den Hochkulturen der Alter Welt, ed. by Dieter Kuhn and Helga Stahl (Heidelberg: Edition Forum, 2001), 85–91.

122 Foster, *Age of Agade*, 260 and 270; Westenholz, *Legends*, 173–87. A third core topic has been identified in the stories about Naram-Sin, namely his "confrontation with an other-than-human barbarian enemy" (Cooper, *Curse of Agade*, 17).

123 But see Westenholz, *Legends*, 173.

124 Foster, *Age of Agade*, 270; Westenholz, *Legends*, 174.

125 Westenholz, *Legends*, 263–368. The original date of composition is unknown, but the story is attested on Old Babylonian tablets, on manuscripts uncovered at Hattusha, the Hittite capital, and on first-millennium Neo-Assyrian and Neo-Babylonian tablets.

126 Westenholz, *Legends*, 264.

127 Westenholz, 'The Old Akkadian Period', 55.

128 The text itself proclaims thus. See Jean-Jacques Glassner, *Mesopotamian Chronicles* (Atlanta, GA: SBL Press, 2004), 263.

129 Glassner, *Mesopotamian Chronicles*, 263–9.

130 *Chronicle of the Esagila*, ll. 62–3.

3   Enheduana the Princess

When she was born, her name was not Enheduana. Presumably, she wasn't even given a name until she had been completely weaned (around three years of age), as the likelihood of survival increased exponentially by then.[1] When this occurred, she was probably given an Akkadian name—like her father Sargon (Sharrukin, "The king is true/firm"), her brothers Rimush ("He is like his/her (i.e., the god Ilaba or the goddess Ishtar) wild bull") and Manishtushu ("Who is with him?"), and her grandnephew Naram-Sin ("Beloved of the god Sin").[2]

Enheduana's family spoke an East Semitic language we call Akkadian. However, since Enheduana lived most of her life in the south, she certainly was bilingual—having learned Sumerian—if not multilingual by the time she died. And she might have very well been bilingual since birth. As for the name by which we know her, it is Sumerian. It means "The high priestess is the adornment of the sky/An," and it was given to her (or she might have chosen it) when she was installed as the high priestess of the moon god Nanna/Sin at Ur.[3]

The history of Sumerian-Akkadian language contact, the mutual influence they had on one another, and the nature of bilingualism during the Sargonic period are complex topics that cannot be satisfactorily treated here.[4] For the purposes of the present investigation, one should note that the Sargonic

> elite used both Akkadian and Sumerian. Rather than making distinctions on the basis of spoken or native language, they often wrote to each other in Akkadian, but when they wrote to the king they preferred Sumerian … In day-to-day activity, Akkadian record-keepers wrote both languages, sometimes in the same document.[5]

The extent to which these written sources reflect the dynamism and the use of the spoken languages of the time is difficult to ascertain, however.

Enheduana was the daughter of Sargon of Agade as she proudly proclaims in the only surviving inscription she commissioned:

DOI: 10.4324/9781032641164-3

Enheduana the Princess 37

Enheduana, *zirru* of Nanna, wife of Nanna, daughter of Sargon, [king] of the world, in [the temple of the goddess Inan]a.ZA.ZA in Ur, made an altar (and) named it: "altar, table of the god An" (or of the sky).[6]

While her religious titles preceded her filiation, she still considered the latter a fundamental part of her identity.

Enheduana was either the half or full sister of Rimush and Manishtushu, Sargon's sons and successors.[7] It is unknown whether Enheduana was older or younger than either of her brothers, and whether they shared the same mother. At present, only one wife is attested for Sargon of Agade. Her name was TashLULtum (meaning and reading unclear), and only one fragmentary document survives, stating that she was Sargon's wife.[8]

Whether TashLULtum was Enheduana's mother (or Rimush's and Manishtushu's) is unknown. She might not have been Sargon's principal wife or the queen, since we do not know whether the Sargonic rulers practiced polygamy or had concubines as other Mesopotamian kings did. To further complicate matters, the heir to the throne need not be the son of the king's principal wife, if he had one.

Our knowledge of Sargonic royal wives is admittedly limited. Currently, we are aware of only two: TashLULtum, wife of Sargon, and Tuta'sharlibbish, wife of Shar-kali-sharri. Since the name of the latter means "She has found the king of her heart," she likely assumed it on the occasion of her betrothal or marriage, a practice attested elsewhere in Mesopotamian history.[9] This interpretation is not universally accepted, however, since a woman by the name of Tuta'sharlibbish is listed in Eshnunna administrative texts from the reign of Naram-Sin.[10] It is possible that she was already betrothed or married to the crown prince at this time. Notably, in the seal impression of one of her majordomos, Tuta'sharlibbish was labeled "the king's beloved."[11] The meaning of this epithet is difficult to ascertain, but we should not assume it was a synonym for "favorite."

To return to Enheduana, a name that we will use since we have no alternative, we do not know where she was born. The most obvious candidates are Agade, her father's capital, or Kish, where Sargon began his career according to later traditions (Chapter 2). Yet, Sargon campaigned heavily not just in northern and southern Mesopotamia but also against Elam and Marhashi in the east, and Magan in the southeast.[12] Sargonic rulers traveled with their families as evidenced from documents dating to the reigns of Naram-Sin and Shar-kali-sharri.[13] As such, Enheduana could have been born pretty much anywhere.

While Enheduana's birthplace is unknown, we can establish her approximate date of birth. She was appointed to the office of high priestess not long after Sargon's conquest of southern Mesopotamia around 2292 BCE. By then, Sargon had been king of Agade for at least 18 years, possibly longer.[14] How old Enheduana was at the time of her appointment is unknown, but she

38 *Enheduana*

must have been relatively young. While it has been suggested that she was around 20 years of age, she could in fact have been younger.[15] Indeed, since Enheduana was ostensibly alive around 2230 BCE, during the Great Revolt, 20 must be considered the upper limit. She was therefore not born much earlier than c. 2312 BCE, but likely in the last decade of the twenty-fourth century BCE (c. 2310–2300 BCE).

Another reason speaks to this date: under the Sargonic Dynasty, two fates befell royal daughters, usually at the will of their fathers. They were appointed to important religious offices, or they were married to foreign rulers to strengthen diplomatic alliances. In both cases, the decision must have occurred when they were young—at the latest by the onset of their first menarche to take full advantage of their reproductive years. To be sure, we have little evidence of marriage practices and women's age at marriage from the Sargonic period. In part, therefore, this reconstruction relies on information from later periods, specifically first-millennium-BCE data indicating that Mesopotamian women typically married between the ages of 14 and 20.[16] While this approach is admittedly problematic, since one runs the risk of attributing to a group of people customs they did not have, there is no reason to believe this practice did not apply to Sargonic women as well.

Evidence for Sargonic royal daughters installed in religious offices is not limited to Enheduana. During his reign, Naram-Sin appointed three of his daughters, Tuttanabshum, Enmenana, and Shumshani, as high priestesses of Enlil at Nippur, Nanna at Ur, and Utu at Sippar, respectively.[17] At least two of these events were commemorated in Naram-Sin's year names, denoting their ideological significance.[18] In both cases, the process included an oracular decision, for instance, "Year when the high priestess of Nanna/Enlil was appointed by the oracle" (Chapter 4).

Iconographic evidence exists for Tuttanabshum (Akkadian for "She is constantly pleasing him").[19] The seal of Aman-Ashtar, her female servant, displays mistress and servant together.[20] The image portrays Aman-Ashtar standing before a female figure seated in front of a tree. The seated woman is not a goddess—no divine attributes are present—but likely Tuttanabshum herself.[21] Depicted in a flounced dress that covers her entire body, the high priestess also wears a headdress. Her long hair falls on her back as she looks forward, seemingly listening to Aman-Ashtar, who is holding an unidentified object, perhaps a musical instrument.

Other Sargonic royal daughters were married off to political allies. Taram-Agade (Akkadian for "She loves Agade"), daughter of Naram-Sin, was likely married to the king of Urkesh.[22] Fragments of her seal impression were uncovered in the royal palace of Urkesh.[23] The inscription is succinct but informative: "Naram-Sin, the king of Agade, Taram-Agade, his daughter." While the seal does not specify that Taram-Agade was married to the ruler of Urkesh, it is likely that her presence at the northern Syrian polity was connected to her marriage and not her appointment into a local religious office.[24] Particularly,

Enheduana the Princess 39

the choice of a contest scene depicting a human-like creature and an animal "is one of the indications of her political position as queen in the Urkesh court."[25]

Another daughter of Naram-Sin involved in an interdynastic marriage was Simat-Ulmash (Akkadian for "The Ornament of Ulmash," a minor deity). A bronze vessel bearing her name was uncovered in Mari.[26] The inscription reads: "Naram-Sin, king of the four quarters, Simat-Ulmash (is) his daughter."[27] It is possible that Simat-Ulmash was married to a Mariote ruler or to a powerful Mariote ally. However, one cannot dismiss the possibility that Simat-Ulmash, too, was a priestess. A bowl with the name of her sister Shumshani (Akkadian for "Another/Second Child"), who was the high priestess of Utu/Shamash at Sippar, was also found at Mari.[28]

Naram-Sin himself may have taken a foreign wife.[29] The copy of a treaty between Naram-Sin and an Elamite ruler, written in Elamite and discovered at Susa, records the two monarchs' mutual responsibilities. It also contains the following good wishes for Naram-Sin and his spouse:

> May your wife be fruitful. May the goddess Simut bless her with her command. … May love blossom for you. May your wife bear you a son.[30]

The goodwill that the Elamite ruler displays towards Naram-Sin's wife suggests that she was his daughter, given in marriage to the Sargonic king to strengthen Elam's diplomatic ties with its powerful neighbor.[31] As for the good wishes for a son, they speak of the Elamite ruler's ambition that his own grandson would become, in the future, king of Agade.[32]

Why Enheduana was not married off to a neighboring potentate but rather installed in one of the most powerful religious offices of southern Mesopotamia is unknown. No information survives about selection practices, if any existed, or court-based conversations about the suitability of royal daughters for either position—religious figurehead or local queen. Certainly, relocating to a different city, whether this entailed entering a foreign court or a local religious institution, must have required adaptability, ingenuity, and savviness.

As for Enheduana's death, Old Babylonian scribes who attributed *Inana B* and *Inana C* to her clearly believed it happened after the Great Revolt—she must have survived it long enough to compose the two hymns. Nothing prevents us from accepting this to have been the case, even if we cannot pinpoint the causes and circumstances of her death. Certainly, Enheduana died during the reign of Naram-Sin, who appointed his daughter to the office that had been hers. The birth name of Enheduana's successor is lost to us, but she took the Sumerian name Enmenana.

Enheduana spent most of her childhood with the women of her family. This was the case for all children, independent of sex. Her rearing must have been privileged—for instance, she might have had a nursemaid, and later nannies and even tutors. The use of nursemaids and nannies by royal families is

40 *Enheduana*

well documented in Mesopotamia.[33] An interesting case is that of Zamena, a nursemaid employed by Queen Uqnitum of Urkesh, the city of Taram-Agade, daughter of Naram-Sin, who might have been queen. Two seal impressions found at Urkesh and dated to the Sargonic period belong to Zamena, the wet nurse for a royal child.[34] The glyptic scene depicts Zamena standing before a chair where Queen Uqnitum is seated, holding her child on her lap. This case is unique among Mesopotamian seal impressions and shows us an intimate moment between mother, child, and wet nurse.[35] As for nannies, they are documented in Sargonic times, but later texts suggest how they might have fit into Enheduana's life. Evidence from second-millennium Mari shows nannies rearing royal children who had been weaned, with the bonds between them lasting into adulthood.[36]

One would like to think that Enheduana grew up playing games. This is most likely what happened, even if little evidence survives, especially from the Sargonic period. Archaeological, artistic, and textual sources from disparate periods inform us about a vast array of games.[37] Mesopotamian children played with rattles when they were still very young, and then graduated to balls and sticks, skipping ropes, toy swords and slingshots, and dolls, numerous among them figurines of animals belonging to the local fauna.

Additionally, Enheduana might have learned basic domestic skills. It was part of a woman's education to be familiar with tasks such as textile work and managing a household. Elite women could also own property, including land, and carry out their own transactions. However, the extent to which this was true for Enheduana before her installation as high priestess is unclear. On the one hand, evidence exists that Sargonic royal women owned their own domains, which were run by administrative officials.[38] On the other hand, there is no data for Enheduana's involvement in such practices.

Thorny is the issue of Enheduana's literacy in her native tongue, Akkadian, and in Sumerian, which she knew regardless of her alleged authorship.[39] To be sure, Enheduana need not have been literate to compose poetry, which could have been transcribed by a scribe.[40] Alternatively, she may have had some training in cuneiform, but it need not have been exhaustive. In Mesopotamia, three levels of literacy existed: functional, technical, and scholarly.[41] Functional literacy allowed the writer to use cuneiform for practical purposes, whereas technical literacy was the realm of certain specialists, such as physicians and diviners. Scholarly literacy was the comprehensive knowledge of cuneiform, which reached the highest levels as the script was studied for its own sake.[42] Functional or technical literacy may have sufficed for Enheduana.

Even if Enheduana was trained in the scribal arts, she probably did not share most pupils' experiences. Whatever training she might have received occurred either wherever she grew up, or in the Ur temple complex where she resided for most of her life. Unfortunately, very little data survives to help us understand Enheduana's circumstances, so we must turn to the documentation about Sargonic scribal education at large to glimpse what Enheduana

Enheduana the Princess 41

might have studied during her training. Before doing so, however, it is important to clarify the linguistic situation of southern Mesopotamia during the Sargonic period, as this impacts Enheduana's own knowledge of languages.

Members of Sargon's family, as well as the Akkadian ruling elite, were at least bilingual. They spoke Akkadian and Sumerian. Two other Semitic languages—Eblaite and Amorite—were in use in Mesopotamia at this time, but more existed.[43] This made the region's linguistic landscape fluid and multi-faceted. None of these languages, however, ever reached the spread that Akkadian did.[44] Furthermore, while "other varieties of the East Semitic dialect continuum were also reduced to writing," only the so-called "language of Akkade" is widely attested, together with Sumerian, in the written documentation dating to the Sargonic period.[45]

The "language of Akkade" was used in contemporary royal inscriptions, numerous administrative texts, as well as correspondence. It eventually became the administrative language of the Sargonic empire, one of many innovations which included "the creation of a standardized script with calligraphic sign form (…) [and] the leading position of scribes in the administrative hierarchy."[46] Sumerian continued to be used and taught, but it remained multi-purposed, as evidenced, for example, by Sargonic Nippur documents.[47]

To write Akkadian, Sargonic scribes adopted and adapted the cuneiform script originally used to encode Sumerian.[48] This script is not alphabetic, but logo-syllabic. This means that each of the several hundred attested signs can represent a word (for example **dumu**, "son"), a syllable (for example **tur**, for which the same sign as **dumu** is used), or both (for example the sign AN, which can be the noun **an**, "sky," or **diŋir**, "god," but also the syllable -an- in the name En-he-du-**an**-na). The system is complex, and its mastery required time and effort.

Scribal education during the Sargonic period is not particularly well documented. Only around 300 school tablets have been identified from cities such as Adab (mod. Bismaya), Girsu, Kish, Nippur, Umma, and Ur in the south, and Ashur, Eshnunna, Gasur, Mari, Nagar, and Tell Leilan in the north and east. However, more than a fourth of the extant tablets have appeared on the antiquities market, and their provenance is unknown, presenting challenges to modern scholars.[49] Moreover, school tablets are not dated, rendering it impossible to discern when during the Sargonic period pedagogical changes were introduced.

Some preliminary conclusions can be drawn, however. Sargonic scribal education occurred in both Sumerian *and* Akkadian along geographical lines. In the south, where Sumerian had been the spoken and written language since at least the early third millennium BCE, education continued in Sumerian. In the north, education was carried out in Akkadian. In other words, there was a concerted effort to teach the local language, whose usage is reflected in the local administrative practices.[50]

42 *Enheduana*

There existed no codified Sargonic scribal curriculum in place across all the regions the Sargonic rulers occupied. Rather, "ad-hoc exercises were the norm," and scribal education seemingly occurred in apprenticeships to train future administrators.[51] Indeed, most school tablets for which we have a confirmed archaeological context have been uncovered in palaces.[52]

Relatedly, Sargonic scribal education "was centered around the administration, and functioned chiefly to train individuals to function as administrators for the institutions of the empire."[53] This should not come as a surprise given the nature and relevance of the "language of Akkade." The technology of writing, too, underwent a transformation—in the stylus, the physical shape, and the spatial organization of tablets.[54] The change in sign orientation, which turned 90 degrees counterclockwise sometime during the second half of the third millennium BCE, might have occurred during this period.[55] These innovations needed to be shared with state administrators, even when scribal practices continued to be carried out in Sumerian.

Cuneiform education began with the basics: how to fashion a tablet from a lump of clay; how to make and hold a stylus; how to impress the stylus in the clay; how to organize the layout of the tablet and the signs on it.[56] Thereafter, pupils learned the basics of cuneiform through the study of sign lists like Syllable Alphabet A. Introduced during the Sargonic Dynasty, the latter became one of the many important tools of early education during the nineteenth and eighteenth centuries BCE.[57]

Upon acquisition of the sign repertoire, students built their vocabulary by studying thematic lexical lists.[58] Some of these consisted of ad-hoc exercises organized around a similar thematic principle.[59] None of the lists that fall under this rubric were used in later periods; nonetheless, their content anticipates second millennium practices. Sumerian and Akkadian personal name lists are attested, as are lists of wooden and metal objects, aromatics, divine names, and toponyms.[60]

Once they had mastered signs, basic vocabulary, and simple sentence structure through the study of personal names, students might have moved on to studying mathematics and metrology—crucial tools in an administrator's arsenal.[61] Model contracts were also part of Sargonic education.[62] While the evidence is limited to a handful of tablets, including administrative texts and records of exchanges, this phase must have been fundamental in familiarizing pupils with the documents they would most frequently compile. Indeed, by mastering contracts and administrative documents, the pupils reached the functional literacy needed to work in the state apparatus.

Scribal education continued with Sumerian and Akkadian literature, which for the Sargonic period is only attested on school tablets. Its purpose of study might have been to further practice the skills already acquired.[63] If other goals were intended, the extant data does not allow us to identify them.

Enheduana the Princess 43

Sargonic literature included royal and votive inscriptions, proverbs and riddles, and incantations.[64] The existence of narrative texts is more difficult to ascertain. Consider the following example:

> The king
> reached the mountain.
> Naram-Sin,
> the king's eldest son,
> covered it with a great net.[65]

This Sumerian document of unknown provenance could certainly be a narrative text. It could also be an excerpt of a royal inscription detailing a ruler's expedition in a mountainous region. Alternatively, this could be an excerpt of a royal hymn, the only example of its kind, as royal hymns are otherwise only attested during the Third Dynasty of Ur and the Old Babylonian period.[66]

Sargonic scribal education seemingly culminated with the study of traditional lexical lists composed during the Early Dynastic period. Indeed, these texts continued to be studied for centuries thereafter, despite their obsolescence—or precisely because of it.[67] Upon completion of this stage, a scribe acquired scholarly literacy.

To conclude, there was ample room for Enheduana to be trained in the scribal arts. Indeed, since she was bilingual, she might have learned to read and write Sumerian *and* Akkadian. While the matter of her literacy might never be settled, there was certainly an infrastructure in place during her lifetime that would have allowed her to become proficient in Sumerian and Akkadian.

Literacy would have served Enheduana well not simply in connection with her alleged poetic endeavors. It might also have empowered her to have a firmer grasp on the vast estate that she controlled as the head of the cult of Nanna in Ur. It is to this cult, and to Enheduana as priestess, that we now turn.

Notes

1 Kristine Garroway, *Children in the Ancient Near Eastern Household* (Winona Lake, IN: Eisenbrauns, 2014), 55.
2 For the meaning of the name Sargon (which was not a throne name), see Schrakamp, 'A View from Within', 612; for Rimush, see Sommerfeld, 'Rīmuš', 372; for Manishtushu, see Steinkeller, 'Man-ištūšu', 334.
3 Wagensonner, 'Between History and Fiction', 39, followed by Kostantopoulos, 'The Many Lives of Enheduana', 58, fn. 2.
4 For an introduction to the topic, see e.g., Jan Keetman, 'Bilingualismus in Sumer zum Gebrauch des akkadischen und sumerischen in der Verwaltungspraxis des Reiches von Akkad unter Narām-Sujēn und Šar-kali-šarrī', *RA* 108 (2014): 1–14.
5 Foster, *Age of Empire*, 213.
6 RIME 2.1.1.16.

44 *Enheduana*

7 *Sumerian King List*, ll. 272–83.
8 RIME 2.1.1.2001. For the reading and meaning of TashLULtum see Frayne, *Sargonic and Gutian Periods*, 36–7.
9 Frayne, *Sargonic and Gutian Periods*, 198; for a different view, see Westenholz, 'Šar-kali-šarrī', 65.
10 Westenholz, 'Šar-kali-šarrī', 65
11 RIME 2.1.5.2003, ll. 6–7.
12 Michalowski, 'The Kingdom of Akkad in Contact with the World', 707–8.
13 E.g., Nicholas L. Kraus, 'When the King Came Down to Sumer: The Royal Sojourn of Sar-kali-sarrē and the Court of Akkad', *Iraq* 81 (2019): 1–14.
14 Sallaberger and Schrakamp, *History and Philology*, 93.
15 Aage Westenholz, 'Assyriologists, Ancient and Modern, on Naramsin and Sharkalisharri', in *Assyriologica et Semitica: Festschrift für Joachim Oelsner*, ed. by Joachim Marzahn, Hans Neumann, and Andreas Fuchs (Munster: Ugarit-Verlag, 2000), 545–56, 555. For the age of women at marriage, see Martha T. Roth, 'Age at Marriage and the Household: a Study of Neo-Babylonian and Neo-Assyrian Forms', *CSSH* 29, no. 4 (1987): 715–47.
16 Roth, 'Age at Marriage', 737.
17 Enmenana succeeded Enheduana at Ur (Schrakamp, 'A View from Within', 624). For Tuttanabshum, see Nicholas L. Kraus, 'Tuṭṭanabšum: Princess, Priestess, Goddess', *JANEH* 7, no. 2 (2020): 85–99.
18 These include the installation of Tuttanabshum as the high priestess of Enlil at Nippur (Sallaberger and Schrakamp, *History and Philology*, 49) and the installation of Enmenana as the high priestess of Nanna at Ur (Sallaberger and Schrakamp, *History and Philology*, 45).
19 The "him" in her name could refer to a deity (in this case Enlil) or to her father Naram-Sin.
20 RIME 2.1.4.2017.
21 For Tuttanabshum's alleged divine status, see Kraus, 'Tuṭṭanabšum', 93–6.
22 Buccellati and Kelly-Buccellati, 'Tar'am-Agade', 11–31. Taram-Agade might have been her birth name, or the name she took when she married the Urkesh king to underline her heritage (Foster, *Age of Agade*, 22).
23 Buccellati and Kelly-Buccellati, 'Tar'am-Agade', 12–3.
24 Buccellati and Kelly-Buccellati, 'Tar'am-Agade', 13–5.
25 Kelly-Buccellati, 'Uqnitum and Tar'am-Agade', 187.
26 Foster, *Age of Agade*, 22.
27 RIME 2.1.4.52.
28 André Parrot, 'Les Fouilles de Mari, Dixième campagne (Automne 1954)', *Syria* 32, nos. 3/4 (1955): 185–211, 192.
29 Foster, *Age of Agade*, 21–2.
30 Translation after Foster, *Age of Agade*, 172.
31 Foster, *Age of Agade*, 172.
32 We do not know if the Elamite ruler got his wish. No extant documents preserve the name of Shar-kali-sharri's mother. It is also worth noting that there is a high likelihood that an Elamite spouse would have been given an Akkadian name upon the occasion of her marriage.
33 Fumi Karahashi, 'Royal Nurses and Midwives in Presargonic Lagash Texts', in *The First Ninety Years. A Sumerian Celebration in Honor of Miguel Civil*, ed. by Lluis Felíu, Fumi Karahashi, and Gonzalo Rubio (Berlin: De Gruyter, 2017), 159–71.
34 Giorgo Buccellati and Mary Kelly Buccellati, 'The Royal Storehouse of Urkesh: The Glyptic Evidence from the Southwestern Wing', *AfO* 42/43 (1995/1996): 22–4.

Enheduana the Princess 45

35 Agnès Garcia-Ventura and M. Erica Couto-Ferreira, 'Nodrizas y lactantes en el Próximo Oriente Antiguo', *Dialogues d'histoire ancienne. Supplément* 19, no. 1 (2019): 31–46, 32–4.

36 Nele Ziegler, 'Les enfants du palais', KTÈMA 22 (1997): 45–57.

37 Anne Draffkorn Kilmer, 'Games and Toys in Ancient Mesopotamia', in *Actes du XIIe Congrès International des Sciences Préhistoriques et Protohistoriques*, 4 volumes, ed. by Juraj Pavúk (Bratislava: Institut archéologique de l'académie Slovaque des sciences, 1993), 359–64.

38 Benjamin R. Foster, 'Notes on Women in Sargonic Society' in *La Femme dans le Proche-Orient antique*, ed. by Jean-Marie Durand (Paris: Éditions Recherche sur les Civilisations, 1987), 53–61, 53.

39 Foster, *Age of Agade*, 206.

40 Kraus, *Scribal Education*, 171.

41 Niek Veldhuis, 'Levels of Literacy', in *The Oxford Handbook of Cuneiform Culture*, ed. by Karen Radner and Eleonor Robson (Oxford: Oxford University Press, 2011), 68–89.

42 Veldhuis, 'Levels of Literacy', 74.

43 Eblaite was an East Semitic language attested in the royal archives of the Syrian city of Ebla during the twenty-fourth century BCE. Whether Eblaite was a separate language or a dialect is a matter of debate (see Michael P. Streck, 'Eblaite and Old Akkadian', in *The Semitic Languages. An International Handbook*, ed. Stefan Weninger et al. [Berlin/Boston: De Gruyter, 2011], 340–58). Amorite, another language in use in the mid-to-late third millennium BCE, survives only through personal names and loanwords attested in Sumerian and Akkadian documents.

44 Walther Sommerfeld, 'Old Akkadian', in *History of the Akkadian Language* (2 vols), ed. by Juan-Pablo Vita (Boston/Leiden: Brill, 2021), 513–665, 515–6 and 554.

45 Sommerfeld, 'Old Akkadian', 555. This language of Akkade (or Agade) is different from Old Akkadian, a practical term "subsuming the remains of the manifold East Semitic dialects found in the cuneiform documentation, from the time of the invention of the script in the fourth millennium down to the beginning of the second millennium" (Sommerfeld, 'Old Akkadian', 513). Thereafter, Old Babylonian was in use in southern Mesopotamia, while Old Assyrian is attested in northern Mesopotamia and Anatolia.

46 Sommerfeld, 'Old Akkadian', 565.

47 Aage Westenholz, *Old Sumerian and Old Akkadian Texts in Philadelphia Chiefly from Nippur. Part One: Literary and Lexical Texts and the Earliest Administrative Documents from Nippur* (Malibu: Undena Publications, 1975).

48 Sommerfeld, 'Old Akkadian', 556–65.

49 Kraus, *Scribal Education*, 7. For tablet distribution see Table 1 on p. 9.

50 Kraus, *Scribal Education*, 179.

51 Kraus, *Scribal Education*, 169, 184.

52 Kraus, *Scribal Education*, 168–9.

53 Kraus, *Scribal Education*, 184.

54 Kraus, *Scribal Education*, 14–5; for the changes in the stylus, see Michele Cammarosano, 'The Cuneiform Stylus', *Mesopotamia* XLIX (2014): 53–90.

55 Kraus, *Scribal Education*, 31–9.

56 Kraus, *Scribal Education*, 14–21.

57 Kraus, *Scribal Education*, 41–8.

58 Kraus, *Scribal Education*, 48–9.

59 Kraus, *Scribal Education*, 49–50.

60 Kraus, *Scribal Education*, 50–80.

61 Kraus, *Scribal Education*, 80–105.

46 *Enheduana*

62 Kraus, *Scribal Education*, 106–12.

63 Kraus, *Scribal Education*, 138.

64 Kraus, *Scribal Education*, 112.

65 CUSAS 26, 270, l. 1–6. The name of the king is not preserved. It is therefore unclear whether Rimush or Manishtushu is meant here.

66 For CUSAS 26, 270 as a royal hymn, see Foster, *Age of Agade*, 208.

67 Kraus, Scribal Education, 138–58; Niek Veldhuis, 'Guardians of Tradition: Early Dynastic Lexical Texts in Old Babylonian Copies', in *Your Praise is Sweet: A Memorial Volume for Jeremy Black from Students, Colleagues, and Friends*, ed. by Heather D. Baker, Eleanor Robson, and Gabor Zólyomi (London: British Institute for the Study of raq, 2010), 379–400.

4 Enheduana the Priestess

Introduction

By the time Enheduana was in her teens, her father had defeated Lugalzagesi of Uruk and incorporated southern Mesopotamia into his realm. This might have been celebrated with pomp and circumstance not just in Agade, where Enheduana might still have resided, but elsewhere in the kingdom. Certainly, Sargon considered his victory so significant that he commissioned royal inscriptions commemorating it.[1] These were inscribed on steles displayed in the many sanctuaries of the land. Some were erected in Enlil's temple in Nippur, where later scribes copied them, considering them excellent examples of the genre.

The steles were decorated with images of epochal events. An example was uncovered in Susa, the Elamite capital, where it had been taken by King Shutruk-Nakhunte (r. c. 1184–1155 BCE) when he sacked Mesopotamia in the mid-twelfth century (Figure 4.1).[2] On it, Sargon holds a net containing his defeated enemies. The head of one sticks out: his body is naked, trapped in the net; his hair is disheveled, and Sargon, a much larger figure, smites him with his mace. This wretched captive is Lugalzagesi, the once mighty king of all lands, now defeated, humiliated, and paraded around for all to see—a message of power, and a warning that a new overlord was in charge.[3] Enheduana was soon to become one of his most powerful representatives.

The City of Ur

Ur (Sumerian and Akkadian **Urim**, written **ŠEŠ.AB.KI** 𒌷𒀭𒀭) was the city of the moon god—literally. The logogram used to write its name (𒌷𒀭, **URI₅**) combines two cuneiform signs representing the moon god Nanna (𒀭, **ŠEŠ**) and a term most likely designating "space" (𒀊, **AB**).[4] The area that became the settlement and later the city of Ur was occupied from the Ubaid period (c. 5800–4000 BCE), if not earlier.[5] Its location, close to the Euphrates River, the sea, the marshes, and the steppe, made it especially suitable for human occupation, as different ecological niches allowed for agriculture,

DOI: 10.4324/9781032641164-4

48 *Enheduana*

Figure 4.1 Sb 2/6053. Drawing of the Stele of Sargon, Sargonic Period. From Susa. Courtesy of Lorenzo Nigro.

animal husbandry, and hunting and gathering. Once writing was introduced, the name of the city appears in documents dating to the Uruk period, Phase III (c. 3100–2900 BCE).[6] Ur was continuously inhabited for more than 5,000 years, well into the Hellenistic period (323–30 BCE), when a shift in the course of the Euphrates left the city without direct access to water.[7] In ancient times, the

Enheduana the Priestess 49

sea levels of the Persian Gulf were higher, placing Ur much closer to it than its remains are now. Archaeological and architectural evidence is scarce for the formative phases of Ur's development. During the Ubaid period, people at the site lived in a seemingly self-sufficient egalitarian society. Their abodes were made of reed and mud; if more substantial buildings existed, they were in areas of the city that have not been excavated. Likewise, no temples have yet been uncovered dating to the Ubaid period, although they are attested elsewhere, for example at Uruk and Eridu (mod. Tell Abu Shahrain).[8]

Data from Ur is limited for the fourth millennium (Uruk period), which saw the emergence of urbanism in Mesopotamia. At this time, Uruk, which lies about 50 miles northwest of Ur, became a major metropolis with extensive cultural and commercial contacts within and outside Mesopotamia.[9] Ur had more modest dimensions, not reaching more than 25 hectares in size (0.25 square kilometers) during the late fourth and early third millennia BCE.[10] Evidence for religious architecture dating to this period has been identified underneath the remains of the ziggurat that Ur-Namma (r. c. 2112–2094 BCE) commissioned in the twenty-first century BCE.[11] The architectural remains do not allow us to reconstruct how this early iteration of Nanna's temple might have looked. Documents suggest that Ur was part of a regional network centered around Uruk, and under its influence.[12]

Beginning in the Early Dynastic period, Ur flourished as a powerful city-state controlling its hinterland and capable of fully exploiting its natural resources.[13] Archaeological and written records from the early third millennium, although limited, show that Ur continued growing and that a complex administrative system was in place.[14] Ur's leader acted as the representative of the poliad god Nanna.[15] This ruler used the title **lugal**, regularly translated as "king"—one of three titles that defined Early Dynastic authority.[16] A few documents in the name of these Ur officeholders survive, but date to the mid-third millennium BCE.[17]Evidence for a central precinct dating to this period exists, although whether it was a temple or the seat of the ruler of Ur, separate from the priesthood, is unclear.

By then, Ur reached around 50 hectares in size. Still independent, the city prospered, and the central precinct was rebuilt. We understand Ur's history better because written texts are more abundant, as are archaeological remains. It was under the leadership of the so-called First Dynasty of Ur that the Cemetery of Ur was constructed.[18] Although most of its burials are relatively simple, 16 tombs housed the remains of the local kings and queens, who were buried with much wealth and pomp.[19] Some of these rulers are attested in the *Sumerian King List*, which inspired the modern moniker "First Dynasty of Ur."[20] This dynasty was in power for about 150 years (twenty-sixth to twenty-fifth centuries BCE), and the richness of its kings' tombs attests to its engagement in local and long-distance trade, in particular with the inhabitants of Meluhha in the Indus River Valley.[21]

50 *Enheduana*

Not long after the end of the First Dynasty of Ur, Uruk gained control of the city (c. 2450 BCE or thereafter). Ur's dependence on Uruk continued up to and including the reign of Enshakushana of Uruk. Thereafter, the city fell first under Lugalzagesi's control and then under Sargonic domination.

Archaeological remains pertaining to the Early Dynastic Nanna temple complex are available. This is a fortunate happenstance, as it was standard practice for builders to enclose "older religious buildings inside or below later models because they were too holy to destroy."[22] The late Early Dynastic sanctuary of Nanna was erected on a human-made terrace, possibly even a ziggurat, albeit smaller than its later counterpart. At least three buildings might have been erected on this terrace: besides Nanna's temple, one to Ningal, his spouse, might have existed, as well as an edifice for the preparation of the deities' meals.[23]

Archaeological evidence for Sargonic Ur is limited because Nanna's sanctuary was reconfigured during the Third Dynasty of Ur. Epigraphic evidence is more forthcoming. Sargon claimed to have destroyed Ur's city walls in the inscription celebrating his victory over Lugalzagesi.[24] So did Rimush when Ur rebelled against him during his first regnal year.[25] Yet, upon returning from his campaign against Elam and Marhashi, Rimush dedicated several objects from the booty to Nanna in Ur.[26] If he commissioned any work for the temple complex, he does not tell us.

Rimush's brother Manishtushu erected monuments in Ur in connection to his campaign against Anshan (mod. southwestern Iran). The evidence consists of an Old Babylonian tablet that was a copy of Manishtushu's standard inscription about the event.[27] However, the author of the tablet most likely copied the inscription from the original, which was inscribed on a statue or a stele in the temple of Nanna.[28] Whether Manishtushu's generosity extended to working on the Nanna complex itself is unclear.

The case of Naram-Sin is more complex since it was during his reign that Lugal-Ane of Ur allegedly elevated himself to kingship in Ur and expelled Enheduana from her residence, and possibly from Ur itself. Naram-Sin likely wreaked havoc in Ur to quash the rebellion. Yet, like Rimush, he dedicated booty from Magan to the moon god at Ur.[29] Furthermore, he dedicated a statue of Nanna/Sin in Ur, as evidenced from later copies of the text inscribed on the statue.[30] It is unclear whether these dedications occurred before or after the Great Revolt and whether Naram-Sin demolished Ur's walls, as Sargon and Rimush claim to have done.

Naram-Sin was an active temple builder. While his magnum opus might have been the (re-)building of the temple of Enlil at Nippur, he also built (or, most likely, rebuilt or repaired) the temple of Nanna/Sin at Ur; both temples were crucial to the Sargonic ideology of kingship.[31] These projects need to be situated in the broader context of Naram-Sin's building program, which also included other sanctuaries.[32] It is also possible that Naram-Sin's interventions in Ur—the construction of the temple, the dedication of a statue of the god,

Enheduana the Priestess 51

and even of the booty from Magan—related to the installation of his daughter Enmenana to Ur's highest religious office.

Naram-Sin died before he was able to complete Enlil's temple at Nippur, a task that fell upon his son and successor, Shar-kali-sharri.[33] Like his predecessors, Shar-kali-sharri carried out building activities, but evidence of his involvement in Ur is non-existent. Indeed, by the end of Shar-kali-sharri's reign, Ur might have regained its independence, albeit not for long.[34] The city eventually fell under Lagash's control. Enmenana was succeeded by Enanepada, daughter of Ur-Bau, king of a newly independent Lagash.[35]

Ur continued to be occupied for 2,000 after Enheduana's death, and information about the city abounds.[36] For instance, archives document the activities of the early second millennium BCE ŋipar, and of the Ganunmah, the "Great Storage House," whose functions changed over the centuries.[37] While some of these documents will be used to better understand the inner workings of the temple complex during the Sargonic period, it is important to recognize their limitations, as they postdate Enheduana's time by centuries.

What did Ur look like during Enheduana's life? The city probably surpassed 50 hectares and was enclosed by a mud-brick wall, destroyed at least twice during the Sargonic period. These walls certainly had gates, although how many is unknown. Already operational during Enheduana's lifetime, if not earlier, were harbors located to the north and west of the city.[38] Both must have been vibrant with activity and offered passers-by an opportunity to admire a vast array of boats, goods, and people from neighboring cities and faraway lands.[39]

Mud-brick played a central role in the urban landscape, although stone was used to build the subterranean Early Dynastic royal tombs, as well as certain foundations.[40] Houses, workshops, temples—the Nanna complex was not the only religious area of the city—and the palace that once housed the local leaders were made of sun dried mud-brick.[41] Occasionally, baked bricks, a sign of wealth and status, were employed for these edifices.[42] Other building materials included timber, bitumen, gypsum, and chaff.[43]

Old Babylonian period domestic architectural remains inform us that the area south of the Nanna temple complex was inhabited by people working for the Nanna temple and its associated shrines.[44] We cannot confirm that this spatial organization was in place during Enheduana's lifetime.

A multitude of streets facilitated the circulation of people, animals, and goods. However, the city layout probably lacked organization since Ur had grown slowly over centuries of continuous occupation. Thoroughfares had a ceremonial role in public processions and provided open spaces for civic, economic, and social activities.[45] Streets varied in width and were flanked by houses and businesses such as workshops and taverns.[46] Open spaces, too, must have been a feature of Ur's urban landscape. To be sure, neither public squares nor gardens have been uncovered in *any* Mesopotamian city dating to the third and second millennia—they are attested only in

52 *Enheduana*

documents from the first millennium BCE.[47] Nevertheless, such areas might have been part of Sargonic Ur, which had a system of watercourses capable of supporting gardens inside its city walls.[48] Public works, typically sponsored by the king, for example, Ur-Namma and Sennacherib (r. 705–681 BCE), beautified the city and allowed the ruler to display his mastery over natural forces.[49]

Ur's cemetery was still in use during the Sargonic period. The associated tombs were not royal in nature, nor did they account for the entirety of the city's population. Other burial sites must have existed. People were also interred under their homes, as was the case with Nanna's high priestesses (see below).

The city landscape must have been dominated by Nanna's sanctuary complex and its temple. Elevated from the ground level by means of a terrace or a ziggurat, the shrine would have stood majestic, visible from everywhere in the city. If, like one of its predecessors, it had been coated with white gypsum, the sunlight reflecting off its walls might have blinded viewers.[50] In its shadow, Enheduana spent her adult life.

Mesopotamian Religion: Sumerian and Akkadian

Before delving into the intricacies of Enheduana's duties as high priestess of Nanna/Sin at Ur, a brief introduction to Mesopotamian religion is necessary.[51] As a reminder, northern Mesopotamian people spoke Semitic languages, Akkadian being the best documented.[52] Conversely, the inhabitants of southern Mesopotamia spoke Sumerian, a language isolate; however, Akkadian had probably begun to spread into the south already in the mid-third millennium BCE.[53]

Sumerian and Akkadian speakers worshiped pantheons of deities that had different names but shared similar responsibilities. Thereby, the coexistence of Sumerian and Akkadian speakers led to a process of syncretism through which two deities were identified with one another.[54] This process occurred with numerous deities, but for our purposes two are significant: Inanna/Ishtar and Nanna/Sin.

Inana, the poliad deity of Uruk, was the Sumerian goddess of love and warfare, as well as the embodiment of the planet Venus. Her Akkadian counterpart, Ashtar in Old Akkadian, and Ishtar in later periods, was also the goddess of love and warfare. Inana and Ashtar were syncretized during the third millennium BCE.[55] Inana was the protagonist of at least two works attributed to Enheduana. Ashtar was the patron deity of the city of Agade, and of the Sargonic Dynasty, which in turn might explain Enheduana's devotion to her.[56]

Nanna was the Sumerian moon god, poliad deity of Ur, and he was associated with fertility.[57] His Akkadian equivalent was Sin, with whom he was syncretized as early as the first half of the third millennium BCE.[58] Information about Sin during the Sargonic period is scant, but he must have played a

Enheduana the Priestess 53

significant role. The moon dominated Mesopotamian life, in part because its cycle was the basis for the Mesopotamian lunar calendar. Sin has been identified on Sargonic seals, depicted as a young man wearing a crescent-shaped crown.[59] It was Nanna/Sin whom Enheduana served in her capacity as high priestess.

We are relatively well informed about Sumerian religious practices, gods, and myths thanks to numerous administrative, literary, and religious sources from the third millennium BCE.[60] On the one hand, it is important to recognize the individualism of the various Sumerian city-states, wherein a patron deity was worshiped with their family, while other gods and goddesses played a secondary role. On the other hand, the political fragmentation characterizing southern Mesopotamia before the rise of the Sargonic Dynasty did not translate into religious differentiation. Rather, Sumerian city-states shared a common language, a common script, and analogous religious practices and cultic traditions, so much so that ancient attempts at systematization through god lists—which allowed making order out of the numerous local mores—are documented from the mid-third millennium BCE.[61]

The situation for the earliest phases of Akkadian religion, corresponding to the Sargonic Dynasty, is different.[62] There are currently no Akkadian manuscripts preserving divine hymns or myths. This hinders our understanding of the religion and rituals of the time. Information from personal names, administrative documents, and glyptic art helps us shed light on some aspects of Sargonic religious practices.[63] An excellent example is provided by seals where the sun god Shamash (Sumerian Utu) plays a central role.[64] Unfortunately, the ideological underpinnings are lost to us, so we do not know why Shamash had risen to such prominence.

Other Sargonic religious innovations have been identified. First was the inception of "a systematic, national pantheon of the increasing number of deities worshiped."[65] In other words, it seems that the Sargonic religious elite attempted to make sense of the religious complexities of the conquered territories and tried to harmonize them with their own pantheon. Second, for the first time in Mesopotamian history, the ruling king became a living god.[66] While this seismic change might have applied only to Naram-Sin, it paved the way for future rulers to do the same.[67] Third, the practice of installing members of the royal family to powerful religious offices became widespread. This was not limited to Enheduana and her successors but involved other temples as well. Fourth, the goddess Ashtar rose to prominence due to her association with the rise of Agade, which she protected, and of the family who ruled the land, a trend that happened often in subsequent Mesopotamian history.[68] Finally, extispicy, a divination practice wherein religious specialists interpreted the will of the gods by observing sheep's entrails, might have been introduced during the Sargonic period—or at least during the third millennium BCE.[69]

54 *Enheduana*

Some of these innovations survived the Sargonic rulers. Others that we are currently unable to identify probably did as well. Indeed, the religious situation in Mesopotamia at the time of Enheduana's installation was particularly complex, although it is unlikely that she played a role in its systematization and simplification. This does not, however, diminish her contributions to the office she held throughout her adult life.

The Origins of Enheduana's Office

One of the debates surrounding Enheduana's life has to do with the origins of her office. Enheduana is the earliest named office holder. As such, it has been argued that this office did not exist in the preceding period but was an innovation of Sargon, created to give him a religious and political stronghold in Ur.[70] To be sure, the office that Sargon allegedly introduced was (at least technically speaking) not that of high priestess (Sumerian **en**, Akkadian *entu*) but rather *zirru*, the designation Enheduana used in her only surviving inscription and which means "hen" (see below).[71] The term **en** is attested as early as the late fourth millennium BCE, where it designated the ruler-priest of Uruk.[72] It was only under Naram-Sin that the highest official in Nanna's cult at Ur began using this title.[73]

The notion that Sargon introduced the office of *zirru* of Nanna is not universally accepted. Artistic and epigraphic evidence suggests that it predated Sargon's conquest of the south.[74] A female officiant for the cult of Nanna is documented in an archaic administrative tablet from Ur.[75] In this scenario, Sargon appropriated the office of *zirru* and assigned it to his daughter precisely because it had a long and established history.

As for the title of **en**-priestess (henceforth "high priestess"), there is no evidence that Enheduana ever carried it, except, of course, in her new name.[76] Later documents retroactively bestow the title upon her, but the sole contemporary inscription we possess is unequivocal and states that she was, first and foremost, the *zirru* of Nanna.[77] One document does not an argument make. However, it is worth noting that the Disk of Enheduana, which bears this inscription, became an important relic already in antiquity.[78] Perhaps, it was held in high esteem partly because it harkened back to one of the most illustrious holders of the old and prestigious office of *zirru*, already attested in the Early Dynastic period.[79] Enheduana might have privileged this title above others to ensure the ideological continuity of a well-established tradition.

It was only after Enheduana's death that high priestesses began to use the title "high priestess" together with that of *zirru*. Enmenana, Naram-Sin's daughter and Enheduana's successor, commissioned an inscription that reads: "[Naram-Sin, king of the four quarters]: Enmenana, *zirru* of Nanna, spouse of Nanna, high priestess of Sin at Ur, (is) his daughter."[80] Enmenana, too, privileged the title *zirru*, like her great-great-aunt.

Enheduana's Installation

Presumably, Sargon did not offer Nanna's clergy any choice when it came to installing his own daughter in the highest religious office in Ur. Indeed, it is likely that an existing priestess had to be deposed to make room for the daughter of the new Akkadian overlord. Regardless, certain established procedures must have marked the occasion. Evidence from the reign of Naram-Sin and from the Third Dynasty of Ur indicates that the high priestess was selected by oracles. Year names commemorate the year when "the high priestess of Nanna, daughter of Naram-Sin, was appointed by the oracle" (year unknown) and the year when "Enmahgalana was chosen by means of the omens as high priestess of Nanna" (Amar-Suen 4).[81]

The year names of Shulgi (r. c. 2094–2046 BCE) are particularly informative. Shulgi's 15th regnal year indicated that one of his daughters had been chosen as the high priestess of Nanna through extispicy. At the time of selection, she was given the name Ennirziana, "The high priestess is/has the rightful trust of the sky/An." Since extispicy interpreted divine messages by reading the entrails of sheep and goats, ideologically, the gods selected the office holder, and the diviner conveyed their will to the king.[82] In practice, this decision would have been politically motivated and therefore politically guided.

Oracular selection did not mean immediate installation. While Ennirziana was chosen during her father's 15th regnal year, it wasn't until two years later that she assumed her position. Shulgi's 17th regnal year was the "Year when Ennirziana, the high priestess of Nanna, was installed." This might also have occurred in Enheduana's case. Based on the Ur III evidence, Enheduana might have received or chosen her name at the time of the oracular decision.

The Office of High Priestess

Mesopotamian high priests and priestesses held the most important religious offices in the land.[83] A god's cult was led by a priestess, while a goddess's was led by a priest.[84] Thus, Enheduana served the temple of the moon god at Ur. But what were the responsibilities of her office?

Answering this question requires some familiarity with Mesopotamian temples. They were urban phenomena—no extramural sanctuaries have thus far been unearthed in modern-day Iraq or Syria.[85] This does not mean that sanctuaries lacked open spaces, however. Evidence of courtyards and processional ways exists, though their function, and the events and celebrations staged there, are not easily discerned.

Temples were the earthly abode of a deity. The Sumerian and Akkadian words for temple, e_2/bītum, designate a "house" first and foremost. Each city had a complex dedicated to its poliad deity, as well as temples to other gods. Underpinning the Mesopotamian belief system was the notion that humankind

56 *Enheduana*

had been created to serve the gods. Temples became the place where this could best be accomplished.

The religious complex was a "sanctuary" or "sacred precinct" (Sumerian eš₃/Akkadian *bītum*), and it included all buildings regardless of their function.[86] From at least the late fourth millennium BCE, and certainly by the mid-third, sanctuaries were economic and religious institutions. They produced food and other commodities, collected and processed donations and taxes, and redistributed their accumulated wealth to the community, often in exchange for services. As such, the sacred precinct included not just the temple but also storerooms, granaries, workshops, and, in certain cases, residences for the clergy.

When Enheduana became the high priestess of Nanna, she did not simply acquire cultic responsibilities. She also became the head of a powerful and wealthy estate, at least partly supported by the crown. Like a woman in charge of managing her family's household, Enheduana controlled the temple complex.[87] While the evidence dates to the office of high priestess in the twenty-first century BCE, it could well have applied to the office of *zirru* in the Early Dynastic and Sargonic periods. By virtue of the complexity of Mesopotamian temples, Enheduana's responsibilities must have spanned several realms—religious, economic, political, and social.[88]

Religious Duties

A Mesopotamian temple was a beehive of activities performed by priestly and non-priestly personnel. Menial tasks were assigned to minor staff, while more important ones were the prerogative of the high priestess and other religious figures. One duty that only she could discharge was the sacred marriage ritual, provided, of course, that such a rite took place.[89]

The term "sacred marriage" derives from the Greek *hieros gamos* and refers to the union of Zeus and Hera, the head of the Greek pantheon and his wife.[90] In a Mesopotamian context, this term typically applies to the union between Inana and Dumuzi—Inana's husband and a god associated with shepherds—and/or their earthly representatives. While the king always assumed the role of Dumuzi, Inana's role could be fulfilled by a high priestess or by one of the king's spouses or concubines.[91]

To be sure, evidence for a Mesopotamian sacred marriage is meager. We have no document explicitly stating that such a ritual existed, let alone that it took place on a regular basis. Nevertheless, this rite might have taken place at least during the Third Dynasty of Ur and the early Old Babylonian and Neo-Assyrian periods (912–609 BCE). Furthermore, the rite might date back to the Early Dynastic period, if not all the way to the beginning of Mesopotamian history.[92] Similar uncertainty surrounds the purpose of the ceremony. Whether it was carried out to ensure the fertility of the land, the success and prosperity of the king, both, or neither, cannot be firmly established.[93] It could certainly

Enheduana the Priestess 57

have been a multi-purposeful rite. It is also unlikely that it fulfilled the same function during the third millennium as it did in the first.[94] There is no contemporary evidence that the sacred marriage took place during the Sargonic period. Yet, Enheduana's main title was *zirru*, which means "hen." Ideologically, this transformed her into the earthly hen of Nanna, and so the counterpart of the heavenly hen of Nanna, his wife Ningal.[95] Such an interpretation is confirmed by the second title Enheduana uses on her disk, "spouse of Nanna."[96]

The identification between Enheduana and Ningal emphasized Enheduana's role as a vessel for the communication between the human and divine planes, although it is highly unlikely it made her divine. Moreover, through a (symbolic) physical union with Nanna, Enheduana contributed to creating wellbeing, harmony, and balance in the human realm.[97] Contemporary documents never explicitly mention this, nor do the works attributed to Enheduana, at least directly. Yet, in *Inana B*, Enheduana claims:

I did not defile (Nanna's) flowery bed,
I did not divulge Ningal's words.
I am Nanna's dazzling high priestess.[98]

Enheduana's "flowery bed" (Sumerian ^{ges}nu$_2$ gi-rin-na) has also been translated as "fruitful," or "blossoming."[99] However, the Sumerian terms gi-rin-na and dadag (here translated as "dazzling," an epithet for Enheduana) also indicate purity—presumably meant as ritual purity in this context. As such, a translation, "I did not defile (Nanna's) pure bed (...) I am Nanna's pure high priestess" cannot be discounted. Irrespective of the translation, the mention of a bed might be a reference to the physical locus of the rite, whereupon she enacted a sexual encounter with Nanna himself. Such a locus has been identified in Enheduana's residence.[100]

Other rituals had to be completed as well, at least according to *Inana B*:

I am the high priestess, I am Enheduana.
I carried the basket of offerings; I sang songs of joy.[101]

The mention of offerings comes as no surprise. Temples received a multitude of offerings, some of which went to the feeding of the gods. According to Mesopotamian religious practices, the gods at times resided in their cult statues, which needed to be clothed, washed, maintained, and fed. The gods received at least two meals per day, consisting of two courses including meat and bread, fruit and cake, and beverages like beer, wine, and milk.[102] Feeding the gods was a ritual action and so was accompanied by the performance of music, the fumigation of the table, and the washing of the statue after the meal. Gods were also the recipients of banquets on special occasions.

58 *Enheduana*

Individuals, too, could offer meals to garner favor.[103] Enheduana's tasks might have involved the care and feeding of Nanna's (and Ningal's) cultic statues. Enheduana might have also intoned daily songs to accompany the god's ritual feeding—or other ritual activities. She might have been accompanied by other singers, particularly in more solemn and important occurrences. To be sure, we do not know exactly what constituted these "songs of joy" (Sumerian **asila**). They were not restricted to the cult of Nanna at Ur but were sung in other religious occurrences.

Enheduana must also have been charged with temple maintenance, namely financing and organizing the care and preservation of the sanctuary. This responsibility is, however, evidenced only in later documents. An inscription of a later high priestess, Enanedu ("The high priestess made suitable by An"), who was the daughter of Kudur-Mabuk and sister of two kings in nineteenth–eighteenth century BCE Larsa (mod. Tell as-Senkereh), Warad-Sin (r. c. 1834–1823 BCE) and Rim-Sin I (r. c. 1822–1763 BCE), confirms this.[104] She restored a section of Nanna's sanctuary called the **ŋipar**, the abode of the high priestesses, and the cemetery where the office holders were buried, as described by a foundation cone uncovered in the building.[105] The relevant section reads:

> At that time, the shining **ŋipar**, residence of my office of high priestess, its bricks not fitting their base, I, Enanedu, high priestess, truly called by a supreme name, daughter of Kudur-Mabuk, laid tightly fitting bricks of the shining **ŋipar**. I plastered its walls aligned to a finger. I gave a new form to that house. At that time, the place of the "Hall-that-brings-bitterness", the place of those (who had gone to their) destiny, the former high priestesses, was not surrounded by a wall, its accesses and …[106] had collapsed, and there were no guards (and) the place was not pure. … I established a broad sacred area surpassing the graveyard of the former high priestesses. I surrounded that ruined place with a wall, established a strong watch, and purified that place.[107]

The language and the medium Enanedu employed—a Sumerian inscription on a foundation cone—echo long-standing royal responsibilities vis-à-vis the care of temples in the land. Although undocumented, Enheduana's building activities, driven by the necessity to keep Nanna's sanctuary in good order, might have been extensive.

Enheduana must have undergone purification rites in preparation for ceremonies and as part of her religious duties towards Nanna and Ningal.[108] Ritual purity should not be understood as chastity, however, nor should we assume that high priestesses had to abstain from sex. While information for the Sargonic period is lacking, evidence exists that high priestesses could have children, as was the case for Enanatuma ("The high priestess is suitable for the sky/An"), daughter of Ishme-Dagan, king of Isin (r. c. 1954–1934). She had at least a son according to a seal impression found on two tablets from Ur.[109]

Enheduana the Priestess 59

Enheduana would have overseen religious personnel in the discharge of her duties. Information comes from later administrative documents uncovered in the ŋipar, where Enheduana resided. Besides housing her, her predecessors, and her successors, the ŋipar also contained a temple to Ningal, Nanna's spouse. Unfortunately, the texts date only from the Third Dynasty of Ur and the Old Babylonian period.[110]

One should be skeptical of using documents dating several hundred years after Enheduana's death to understand the complexities of running a Sargonic-period temple. Nevertheless, there exists a remarkable degree of continuity in religious and administrative practices from the mid-third to the early second millennium, even when considering the innovations of the Sargonic dynasts. Thus, it is not too far-fetched to imagine that the temple was similarly run under Enheduana.

Recorded in documents from the reign of Abi-sare of Larsa (r. c. 1841–1830 BCE), we find the **gudu₄**-priests (Akkadian *pašišu*).[111] They fed and cared for the gods, carried out lustration rites, and, when needed, performed labor in the temple.[112] The office is first attested towards the end of the Early Dynastic period and is documented in the Sargonic period as well.[113] It is likely that these officials were employed to serve the temples associated with the ŋipar already during Enheduana's time. Whether these priests are depicted on the Disk of Enheduana, or other priests are, we cannot say. Nevertheless, the disk portrays a series of religious staff, and it should be used to further nuance our understanding of Enheduana's office.

The Disk of Enheduana

The only artistic evidence we possess for Enheduana depicts her fulfilling her religious duties.[114] The Disk of Enheduana (Figure 4.2) was discovered in 1927 in the Isin-Larsa archaeological layers of the ŋipar.[115] Made of alabaster, a white, translucent stone, the disk had been smashed into several pieces in antiquity. Once reconstructed, it revealed an object 25.6 cm wide and 7.1 cm thick.[116] The choice of shape and material suggests that the disk was meant to evoke a full moon, an appropriate symbolism considering the god Enheduana served. Likely, it was commissioned during Sargon's reign, since Enheduana refers to her father as king. This is not certain, however, as she might have preferred to hold onto this title even after he died. "King's Daughter" sounds more illustrious than "King's Sister" or "King's Great-Aunt."

The disk contains a one-register scene on the obverse. The numerous photos of the disk available today are somewhat misleading since they show a restored object. In reality, the image had three, and not four, figures standing before an offering table. Moreover, the ziggurat reconstructed on the left side of the register might not have looked as it does today (Figure 4.3).

60 *Enheduana*

Figure 4.2 Disk of Enheduana, Sargonic Period. From Ur. Courtesy of the University of Pennsylvania Museum of Archaeology and Anthropology, Philadelphia.

The right-most complete figure is a naked male attendant, possibly a priest. His head is shaven, and he holds an object that may be a fly-swatter.[117] Before him is a female figure who is slightly taller than the rest.[118] Universally identified as Enheduana in light of the inscription on the back of the disk, she wears a long tufted dress and an elaborate headdress (Sumerian **aga**$_{(3)}$) often worn by high priestesses.[119] The details are so fine that we can see Enheduana's hair is plaited. Her right hand is raised before her face in a gesture of reverence.[120]

Before Enheduana is another naked male officiant pouring libations from a spouted vessel in front of an altar. This might be the same structure celebrated in the inscription on the reverse: the altar named "table of the god An (or of the sky)."[121] The ritual action performed by the priest and supervised by

Enheduana the Priestess 61

Figure 4.3 Disk of Enheduana before Reconstruction, Sargonic Period. From Ur. Courtesy of the University of Pennsylvania Museum of Archaeology and Anthropology, Philadelphia.

Enheduana occurs before a building, which modern restorers have made into a four-tiered ziggurat. Only traces of two, or possibly three, tiers survive on the disk itself.[122]

The disk's inscription is revealing. Enheduana's religious roles are more important than her filiation, as evidenced by the fact that her titles ("hen of Nanna" and "spouse of Nanna") are listed first. Furthermore, the disk commemorates the construction of an altar for the temple of Inana.ZA.ZA in Ur, and not for the temple of Nanna or Ningal. This indicates that the poorly preserved building which modern restorers envisioned as Nanna's ziggurat might be the temple of Inana.ZA.ZA.[123] She was likely syncretized with the Akkadian Ashtar, the tutelary deity of Agade and of the Sargonic family.[124]

The disk's significance was recognized already in antiquity, as evidenced by its treatment after Enheduana's death. It was uncovered in the Isin-Larsa archaeological layers of the ŋipar, next to a small statue of Enanatuma, daughter of Ishme-Dagan.[125] The statuette was discovered badly damaged and has been poorly restored. It represents a seated woman, Enanatuma herself. She wears a flounced garment, her hair is loose, her head is crowned by a headdress, and her hands are clasped in a pious pose (Figure 4.4). The inscription, located on the chair, reads:

62 Enheduana

Figure 4.4 Statuette of Enanatuma, Old Babylonian Period. From Ur. Courtesy of the University of Pennsylvania Museum of Archaeology and Anthropology, Philadelphia.

For Ningal, prominent lady(?), whose divine powers no divine power can rival, wise counselor, suitable for ladyship, her lady: Enanatuma, high priestess beloved of Nanna, high priestess of Nanna in Ur, daughter of Ishme-Dagan, king of Sumer and Akkade, brought this statue to her bedroom for her. She (=Enanatuma) dedicated it (=the statue) to her (=Ningal) for her own life.[126]

Enanatuma was as significant as Enheduana in the history of the office. As we've discussed, she undertook the restoration of the ŋipar, having found it in disrepair in the aftermath of the fall of the Third Dynasty of Ur. Elamite soldiers had sacked Ur and most likely destroyed the sacred precinct in the process. By using the foundations of the Ur III building, Enanatuma restored the ŋipar to its former glory.[127] This was as much a political move as it was a religious one. Enanatuma's father, Ishme-Dagan, presented himself as the ideological heir to the rulers of the Third Dynasty of Ur, who had completely reconfigured the Nanna temple complex during the twenty-first century BCE.[128] It is not surprising that he appointed one of his daughters to the

Enheduana the Priestess 63

highest religious office in the south and instructed her to restore the ŋipar to its former glory. Enanatuma's mark is everywhere in the ŋipar. Several bricks bearing her name were discovered in its excavation, attesting to her desire to tie herself to its restoration.[129] Furthermore, Enanatuma wished to be associated with her greatest predecessor, Enheduana. This is why she commissioned a votive statuette of herself and deliberately buried it in the foundations of the ŋipar together with the Disk of Enheduana. Damaged and discarded during the Elamite sack, the disk was still ideologically charged: it allowed Enanatuma to connect herself (and her father) well beyond their immediate Ur III predecessors. Indeed, it is entirely possible that it was Enanatuma herself who commissioned a copy of the inscription on the disk be made before the latter was ritually deposed in the foundation of the ŋipar.[130] This ensured the preservation of Enheduana's inscription—and her memory.

Political Role(s)

The authors of the *Sumerian King List* were explicit that rulership was a gift bestowed upon *man*kind. Only one woman is attested in the list: Kug-Bau, the clever tavern-keeper, who became *king*, and not *queen*, of Kish. The message was obvious: kingship was gendered male.[131]

Mesopotamian women traditionally wielded no political power. The one exception is Sammuramat, a ninth-century Assyrian queen who was the wife of Shamshi-Adad V (r. 824–810 BCE). She became regent for her minor son, Adad-nirari III (r. 810–793 BCE), when her husband died.[132] Her success at a time of political instability and dynastic crisis was so awe-inspiring that she was immortalized by classical sources as the famous Semiramis.[133]

As a princess, Enheduana would not have had political sway, even if she'd been married to a local or faraway dignitary. But what about once she became high priestess? To answer this question, we must consider how deeply entwined politics and religion were in Mesopotamia; there existed no separation between "church and state."

The earliest attested Mesopotamian rulers were the priest-kings of Uruk.[134] Even when the notion of managerial and martial leadership emerged in the early third millennium BCE, religion remained a powerful instrument, as the king received his legitimacy by means of his relationship to the gods.[135]

The intimate tie between the ruler and the gods was made explicit in art and royal inscriptions, such as the one commissioned by Eanatum, king of Lagash, in the twenty-fifth century BCE.

> Eanatum, ruler of Lagash, called (to office) by the god Enlil, given strength by the god Ningirsu, chosen in the heart by the goddess Ninhursaga, nourished with the whole milk by the goddess Ninhursaga, endowed with a pleasant name by Inana, granted wisdom by Enki, beloved by

64 *Enheduana*

Dumuzi-Abzu, trusting in Hendursag, beloved companion of Lugal-URUxKAR ... restored the city of Girsu for Ningirsu.[136]

Eanatum and the rulers of his dynasty consistently depicted themselves in close relationships with numerous gods—Ninhursaga, one of the main Sumerian goddesses, was Eanatum's nursemaid! This practice continued in the Sargonic period, when the kings associated themselves with Inana/Ashtar. The dynamics of such relationships were further developed in the ensuing centuries, possibly even through the sacred marriage rite discussed earlier. Thus, kingship retained a strong religious component, and an attempt to separate the two risks attributing to the Mesopotamians ideas not their own. What does this mean for Enheduana? It is generally accepted that:

Sargon deployed elements of the old symbolic system [of the preceding Early Dynastic period] in order to consolidate the Akkadian dynasty's links with the age-old Sumerian customs in the important religious and political center of Ur. This included the strategic placement of his daughter as high priestess of Nanna at Ur.[137]

When Ur was still an independent city, it is likely that the high priestess provided the local ruler with the authority he needed to govern. Therefore, by controlling the office through his own daughter, Sargon could claim to be the rightful king of Ur and gain further legitimacy through Enheduana's blessing of his reign.

Lugal-Ane's alleged actions against Enheduana as recounted in *Inana B* could then be explained through this lens.[138] As Naram-Sin's representative in Ur, Enheduana would not have sanctioned Lugal-Ane's self-elevation to Ur's throne. Similarly, Lugal-Ane's actions might have been perceived as sacrilegious against the local religious establishment, even if the latter considered the Akkadian overlords to be interlopers. By removing Enheduana, Lugal-Ane removed the problem altogether.[139] Consequently, even if Enheduana wielded little to no practical political power, she was a political foil of her family's control over Ur.

Economic Roles

The sanctuary of Nanna at Ur was not simply a religious institution. It was a prosperous economic household controlling many resources—most importantly fertile agricultural land. Unfortunately, the administrative documents it produced during the Sargonic period have not been uncovered. As such, we lack the specifics of the temple's wealth. Nevertheless, Sargonic rulers installed their daughters as high priestesses of local sanctuaries to bring their economic resources under their direct control.[140] In Ur, this must have

Enheduana the Priestess 65

exacerbated the enmity between Enheduana (and her family) and the local elites, whose rights and privileges had been anchored to a long-ago established usage of the land. Particularly frustrated would have been the family who'd controlled the office of high priestess before Enheduana was elevated to it.

Insight into Enheduana's economic power comes primarily from later administrative documents uncovered in the ŋipar. Evidence from the reign of Rim-Sin I of Larsa attests to the existence of an unnamed **saŋŋa**, who acted as the head of the temple administration.[141] This office is well attested elsewhere during the Sargonic period. It is therefore likely that a **saŋŋa** was probably in place during Enheduana's lifetime.[142]

Likewise, a family of temple attendants (Sumerian **šita eš₃**, the "priest of the sanctuary") is documented from the reign of Abi-sare.[143] Their function was religious as well as administrative, and the office goes back to the Early Dynastic period.[144] It is also attested in Sargonic documents, suggesting the possibility that these priestly officials, too, assisted Enheduana. If this was the case, the temple's economic matters might have been handled primarily by the **saŋŋa** and the **šita eš₃**.

A final point is worth making about how later documents can inform us about earlier practices. Enanedu, who held the office when the kings of Larsa ruled over Ur, might have been a money lender.[145] This is not unusual, as lending and other economic activities are well attested for Old Babylonian votive women known as *nadītu*s. Even after having entered the service of Ninurta at Nippur, Marduk in Babylon, or Shamash in Sippar, these women carried out economic transactions including the purchasing and leasing of fields, enslaved people, and houses, as well as money lending.[146] These activities need not have been the purview of the *nadītu*s, nor should they be considered an Old Babylonian phenomenon.

Sargonic documents also survive that provide some insight about Enheduana's possible economic roles. These texts come from two archives uncovered at the Ekur, Enlil's temple at Nippur. Labeled the Onion Archive and the Akkadian Archive, they attest to the temple's economic transactions during the reigns of Naram-Sin and Shar-kali-sharri.[147] The Ekur owned plenty of land dedicated to agricultural production and animal herds. A temple administrator, most likely appointed by the king, managed these assets. The "Onion Archive" provides information about the disbursement of onions, a delicacy cultivated in the Ekur's fields. Illustrious recipients are mentioned, including Princess Tuttanabshum, who was installed as the high priestess of Enlil at Nippur by her father Naram-Sin.[148]

The Akkadian Archive pertains to the rebuilding of the Ekur, a project that Naram-Sin began early in his reign and which was continued by his son and successor, Shar-kali-sharri. The latter was in charge of the archive while he was still a crown prince.[149] The Akkadian Archive provides a window into the daily lives of the people who worked on the project, including manual

66   *Enheduana*

laborers, female weavers, herders, and women employed for grinding barley.[150] Their activities attest to the economic wealth of a religious institution and must have occurred at the Nanna temple in Ur, under Enheduana's supervision, too.

While we do not have the specifics of Enheduana's involvement in any activity or project, we should not dismiss the possibility that she might have overseen temple personnel, carried out economic transactions—both for the temple and in her own name—and supervised work done to the **ŋipar**, as Enanedu did centuries later. It is to this abode that we turn next.

Daily Life: The ŋipar at Ur

Enheduana's daily life was mostly spent inside Nanna's temple complex (Figure 4.5), specifically in the home of the high priestess. This building was called **ŋipar** (written **ŋi₆-par₄**) in Sumerian and *gipāru* in Akkadian, and it is often translated as "cloister."[151] This term is misleading, however, since it evokes ideas about Catholic nunneries that have little to do with Mesopotamia. I opted to leave the term untranslated. In the context of this book, **ŋipar** always refers to the residence of the high priestess of Nanna at Ur, located within Nanna's sanctuary complex.

Little archaeological evidence exists of the **ŋipar** prior to Sargon's conquest of Ur, as the kings of the Third Dynasty of Ur rebuilt the sanctuary extensively.[152] Through this process, earlier buildings were either destroyed or incorporated into new constructions. Even the numerous Sargonic tombs uncovered in the nearby cemetery do not reveal much about life in the **ŋipar**.[153] Yet, the **ŋipar** surely existed during the Early Dynastic period, when the position of *zirru* is first attested, and the Sargonic period, when Enheduana became the office holder.[154]

During the Third Dynasty of Ur, the entire temple complex of Nanna was reimagined. Construction was initiated by Ur-Namma, the founder of the dynasty, finished by his successor Shulgi (r. c. 2093–2045 BCE), and additional work was carried out by Shulgi's successor, Amar-Suen (r. c. 2036–2027 BCE).[155] During this process, the corners of **ŋipar** were aligned with the points of the compass.[156] The **ŋipar** was destroyed by the Elamites, but Enanatuma rebuilt it by following its foundation, as we have seen. This was the structure excavated by early twentieth-century archaeologists (Figure 4.6).

The **ŋipar** was quite large (79 x 76.50 meters). It was located southeast of the Ur ziggurat, just outside its walls. Built in mud-brick, the **ŋipar**'s outer walls were thick and buttressed, and decorated with niches along three sides. Only two entrances have been identified, one of which was flanked by two towers.[157] This suggests a concern with outside attack—and with good reason if Enheduana was removed from her office and, presumably, from the **ŋipar** by force.

Enheduana the Priestess 67

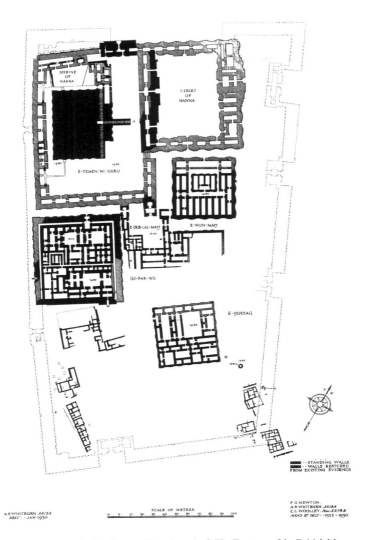

Figure 4.5 Plan of the Ur Ziggurat Complex, Ur. © The Trustees of the British Museum.

68 *Enheduana*

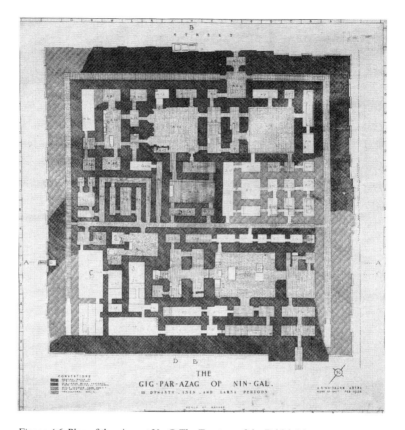

Figure 4.6 Plan of the ŋipar at Ur. © The Trustees of the British Museum.

The building consisted of two main sectors separated by a corridor. The northwestern sector (the top portion of the plan) contained the private quarters of the high priestess, including her living quarters, a private shrine, a storage area, and numerous smaller rooms of unclear function. Underneath some of these rooms, excavators located looted tombs that must have belonged to the high priestesses.[158] This should not come as a surprise since the Mesopotamians often buried their dead below the floors of their houses.[159] The women buried in these tombs received funerary offerings during the Third Dynasty of Ur by means of clay libations pipes.[160] A cemetery was also established by the northeastern wall of the building, which, as we've seen, was enlarged by Enanedu.[161]

Enheduana the Priestess 69

The southeastern sector (the bottom portion of the plan) consisted of the temple of Ningal. The edifice was organized around a large central courtyard and flanked by a kitchen that also served the northwestern sector, and other smaller rooms.[162] These included shrines, a cella that housed Ningal's statue, and storage rooms. One of the rooms in the southeastern sector might have been used in the sacred marriage ceremony.[163] This room was located right next to a niched room with a pedestal upon which Ningal's statue stood.[164]

The height of the building is debated. There is no agreement as to whether a second story was part of the original structure or its successive iterations. To be sure, no stairwells have been unearthed by excavators. Nevertheless, the building's thick walls could have easily supported a second story, at least in some sectors.[165]

Various documents discovered in the ruins of the ŋipar date from the Third Dynasty of Ur to the Old Babylonian period, with the exception of the Disk of Enheduana.[166] These include inscriptions about the rebuilding of the ŋipar, inscriptions on votive objects dedicated to Ningal, and administrative texts.[167] Notably, the administrative documents from the time of Rim-Sin also record the domestic staff employed by the temple. This included a sweeper (Sumerian **kisal-luh**), a doorman (**ne-du$_8$**), a miller (**kin$_2$-kin$_2$**), and the high priestess's guards (**aga-us$_2$ en-na**).[168] The latter indicate a concern for the wellbeing of the high priestess echoed by the fortress-like structure of her residence.

What about Enheduana's personal staff? Surely, she would have had many employees, as she lived in the ŋipar for close to 60 years. Most informative are cylinder seals and seal impressions belonging to four individuals who served in three different capacities. One of them belonged to Enheduana's coiffeur (Sumerian **kinda**), Ilum-palil. Whether he had other responsibilities besides tending to Enheduana's hair, we do not know, and the term is not well attested in the Sargonic period.[169] Ilum-palil's seal was found in his tomb, alongside razors and other blades necessary for his profession.[170] Another seal belonged to Adda, Enheduana's estate manager or majordomo (Sumerian **ugula-e$_2$/šabra$_2$**). The remaining belonged to Sagadu and [x]-kitush-du, Enheduana scribes (Sumerian **dub-sar**).

The identity of Adda is complicated by the uncertainty in interpreting the cuneiform signs of his title. Written **PA.E$_2$**, the title can be normalized as **ugula-e$_2$**, "overseer of the household," or as **šabra$_2$**, "chief administrator" of a temple or other household.[171] Depending on the reading of the signs, therefore, Adda was either the person in charge of Enheduana's household or of the whole temple administration. If he was the overseer of the household (**ugula-e$_2$**), this likely referred to the ŋipar itself and all of the personnel that must have worked therein: cooks and kitchen maids, cleaners and sweepers, laundresses and weavers, and maybe even Ilum-palil the coiffeur, if he and Adda were coevals. Alternatively, Adda might have been the person in charge

70 *Enheduana*

of the *entire* temple administration, thereby acting in lieu of the **saŋŋa** discussed above.

Sagadu and [x]-kitush-du (his name is not fully preserved) were Enheduana's scribes. What this means, however, is unclear. Were they employed to record the administrative transactions of her household and thus part of the personnel either Adda or other majordomos supervised? Did they assist the high priestess in more personal matters?

Daily Life: Enheduana's Experience

How would Enheduana have passed her days?

She woke up at sunrise, having spent the night in her bedchamber, which was probably located in the northeastern corner of the **ŋipar**. We don't know whether she had to perform specific religious rites at daybreak, although this is possible. Among them, one should consider the care and feeding of previous high priestesses buried underneath the floors of the **ŋipar**'s living quarters. While festivals for the dead existed to honor one's deceased relatives, regular food and drink offerings had to be presented as well.[172]

Afterwards, a series of possibilities opened for her: she probably had to meet with her temple officials—religious personnel and administrators alike—to ensure the smooth running of temple matters. If she needed to review tablets, she would have had to go to a courtyard since rooms lacked windows and were poorly lit, or to the flat roofs that covered her abode. The Ur III **ŋipar** had two (A11 and A6 on the plan), and we can imagine her sitting there with baskets of clay and other writing implements, maybe consulting with people like Sagadu and [x]-kitush-du.

By midday, it was time for the first of the two main meals—for her, and for the gods she honored. This is where things get a bit tricky since we do not know whether the temple of Ningal, which consisted of the southeastern part of the **ŋipar**, existed in Sargonic times. Certainly, there would have been small chapels and shrines in the **ŋipar** itself, as there were in later periods.[173] Therefore, Enheduana could have discharged her duties by remaining in the **ŋipar**. But she might have needed to leave the building and reach the temple(s) of Nanna and Ningal, where she would have presented food and drinks before the deities' cult statues. Incidentally, at least from the Ur III period onwards, both human and divine meals were prepared in the **ŋipar**'s kitchen (C32–34).

When Enheduana had to exit the **ŋipar** and venture into the Nanna temple complex, and especially if she went into the city of Ur itself, she would be accompanied by personal guards. After all, Ur was an occupied city after having enjoyed prosperity and independence since the fourth millennium BCE. Most of the population might have been largely unconcerned as to whether their overlord belonged to a long-established line of Sumerian rulers or a

Enheduana the Priestess 71

newly formed northern dynasty. However, the local elite (religious and political) were certainly not content with this situation.

We've already discussed that two major rebellions were quashed brutally—one during Rimush's first regnal year (c. 2276 BCE) and one during Naram-Sin's reign (c. 2230 BCE). But southern Mesopotamia and Ur had been devastated by military actions for decades, well before the rebellion against Rimush led by a self-proclaimed king of Ur by the name of Kaku.[174] After all, both Lugalzagesi and Sargon had campaigned extensively in the region. Rimush claimed to have killed a total of 84,556 men, an impossibly high number. Scholars generally agree, however, that between a quarter and a third of the south's able-bodied men died.[175]

The persistent state of warfare that the people living in Ur experienced must have wrecked families, destroyed societal bonds, and demoralized an entire population. Demoralized, but never broken, if Kaku first and Lugal-Ane 36 years later were willing to risk their lives to regain political independence. Indeed, it seems that as soon as a new generation of men came of age, rebellion against the Sargonic overlords was the inevitable path.

This is the environment in which Enheduana lived. Likely, she was neither well-regarded nor welcomed among the Ur elite, since her relatives were responsible for decimating the families who had joined the opposition to the Sargonic rulership. Even in times of relative tranquility, things may not have been easy in Ur. Data from other southern centers suggests a strong Akkadian presence in conquered cities, potentially a deterrent for local uprisings.

The question is whether the Sumerian cities had autonomy or were directly controlled and integrated into the Akkadian state economy (Chapter 2). While some scholars contend that the southern governors continued to be local, others consider them Akkadian functionaries.[176] To be sure, in centers such as Lagash and Umma, for which Sargonic administrative documents survive, the governor bore a Sumerian name, indicating that he probably belonged to the local elite. These governors appear to have toed the Sargonic line, or at least they pretended to do so, presumably to preserve the privileges their overlords had granted them.[177] If governors were of Akkadian origins, their loyalty might have been guaranteed by their connections with the royal family and by a strong military presence.

Either way, Ur had been an ancient and strong Sumerian center long before Sargon's conquest. It might not have been an easy place for Enheduana to reside. Even with a governor loyal to the Sargonic ruler, the enmity of long-established local families must have been palpable. If she indeed left the ŋipar, she must have been heavily guarded. And as she walked along the numerous streets of Ur, admiring the buildings of earlier times, and the monuments and steles erected by her family to mark its power over the city, she must have also witnessed the scars that ongoing conflict had left on the landscape.

72 Enheduana

Having carried out whatever needed doing outside of the safe perimeter of the ŋipar, Enheduana must have returned to her residence. She might have had to perform additional rituals or supervise household-related matters before her, and the gods' evening meals. Thereafter, she retreated to her quarters to sleep.

It is also worth mentioning that despite our lack of evidence for the Sargonic period, major festivals dedicated to Nanna and Ningal must have been celebrated.[178] What these festivals entailed, and what role Enheduana played in them, is unknown. No Sargonic calendar that might help us shed light on such occurrences has been identified for Ur. Yet, the moon had always been a significant feature in Mesopotamian calendrical matters since its phases dictated the beginning, middle, and end of any given month. Moon festivals are documented from the Third Dynasty of Ur. At this time, one of the most important festivals, called a_2-ki-ti, was dedicated to the moon god Nanna. Celebrated twice a year, during the first and seventh months of the year (corresponding to late March and late September), this festival was connected to agricultural practices.[179] Part of the celebrations took place in the temple of Nanna at Ur, the "House (of) Alabaster" (Sumerian e_2-ŋeš-nu$_{11}$-gal).[180]

Although evidence is indirect, it is likely that the a_2-ki-ti celebration occurred in Early Dynastic and Sargonic Ur as well. Early Dynastic administrative documents from Ur mention the month name a_2-ki-ti, which probably was the time when the festival took place. Similarly, Sargonic documents from Adab, Umma, Zabalam (mod. Tell Ibzheik), and KI.AN (location uncertain) also cite the month of a_2-ki-ti. A Sargonic document from Adab directly mentions the a_2-ki-ti-festival but provides no additional information.[181] Therefore, such a month's name, and its related festival, likely existed at Ur during Enheduana's lifetime.

As for Enheduana's more intimate life—her relationships with her family, her subordinates, and her loved ones, not to mention whether she ever left Ur, at least voluntarily—we know nothing at all. It is doubtful that she ever married, as it would have been incompatible with her role as high priestess. Yet, her position precluded neither personal relationships nor children.

To conclude, the paucity of our sources impedes a thorough reconstruction of Enheduana's daily activities, not to mention insight into her personal life. Nevertheless, the broader context of the times when she lived and the roles that she played aid us in understanding what her life might have looked like. In charge of the most important religious institution in a prominent Sumerian city, Enheduana spent her life as an avatar of Sargonic imperialism. The historical events that she witnessed and the brutality of the wars her family waged must have left a mark on her, as they did on the people of Ur, among whom she spent decades. If, as has been suggested, Enheduana's death occurred not long after the Great Revolt, then her life ended as traumatically

Enheduana the Priestess 73

as it had begun following her father's conquest of the south: surrounded by the destruction her male relatives brought in their ultimately failed attempt at unifying Mesopotamia.

Notes

1 RIME 2.1.1.1–7.
2 Nigro, 'Two Steles of Sargon', 85, fn. 1.
3 Nigro, 'Two Steles of Sargon', 85–93, and Fig. 7.
4 Manuel Molina, 'Ur. A. I. Philologisch. Im 3. Jahrtausend', *RlA* 14 (2014–2016): 354–61, 354. The KI-sign marks what comes before it as a toponym.
5 Harriet Crawford, *Ur. The City of the Moon God* (London/New Delhi/New York/ Sydney: Bloomsbury Academic, 2015), 15–8; Richard L. Zettler and William B. Hafford, 'Ur. B. Archäologisch', *RlA* 14 (2014–2016): 367–85, 368. For the challenges in dating the Ubaid period at Ur, see Crawford, *Ur*, 18.
6 Molina, 'Ur', 354.
7 Crawford, *Ur*, 129–30.
8 Crawford, *Ur*, 16–21, 24–7.
9 Gebhard J. Selz, 'The Uruk Phenomenon', in *The Oxford History of the Ancient Near East: Volume I: From the Beginnings to Old Kingdom Egypt and the Dynasty of Akkad*, ed. by Karen Radner, Nadine Moeller and Daniel J. Potts (Oxford: Oxford University Press, 2020), 163–244. The city might have exceeded 100 ha in size.
10 Molina, 'Ur', 365.
11 Crawford, *Ur*, 38.
12 Molina, 'Ur', 357.
13 Crawford, *Ur*, 48.
14 Walther Sallaberger, 'The City and the Palace at Archaic Ur', in *Shepherds of the Black-Headed People: the Royal Office vis-a-vis Godhead in Mesopotamia*, ed. by Kateřina Šašková, Lukáš Pecha, and Petr Charvát (Plzeň: Západočeská univerzita, 2016), 31–8.
15 Molina, 'Ur', 357; Sallaberger, 'Archaic Ur', 34–5. For the view of the precinct as a temple, see Giuseppe Visicato, *The Power and the Writing – The Early Scribes of Mesopotamia* (Winona Lake, IN: Eisenbrauns, 2000), 13.
16 For **lugal** see eEPSD at: http://oracc.museum.upenn.edu/epsd2/sux, s.v. This term was first attested in ED I-II (https://cdli.mpiwg-berlin.mpg.de/artifacts/453401/ reader/209800). The term **en** was used by the ruler of Uruk (http://oracc.museum .upenn.edu/epsd2/sux); other cities used the title **ensi**$_2$ (http://oracc.museum .upenn.edu/epsd2/sux, s.v.), which came to mean "governor."
17 For example, RIME 1.13.3.1, for which see Frayne, *Presargonic Period*, 385–6.
18 Crawford, *Ur*, 48–9. The cemetery continued to be used until the end of the Sargonic period.
19 Richard L. Zettler and Lee Horne, *Treasures from the Royal Tombs of Ur* (Philadelphia, PA: University of Pennsylvania Museum of Archaeology and Anthropology, 1998); Crawford, *Ur*, 48–51. No consensus exists as to who was buried in the royal tombs. See, e.g., Susan Pollock, 'Death of a Household'. In *Performing Death: Social Analyses of Funerary Traditions in the Ancient Near East and Mediterranean*, ed. by Nicola Laneri (Chicago, IL: The University of Chicago Press, 2007), 209–22; Gianni Marchesi, 'Who was Buried in the Royal Tombs of Ur? The Epigraphic and Textual Data'. *OrNS* 73, no. 2 (2004): 153–97.
20 Frayne, *Presargonic Period*, 377–8.

74   *Enheduana*

21   For the Indus Civilization's exportation of finished carnelian beads during the third millennium BCE, see Robin Cunningham and Ruth Young, 'An Era of Integration: The Indus River Valley Civilization', in *The Archaeology of South Asia: From the Indus to Asoka: c. 6500 BCE–200 CE*, ed. by Robin Cunningham and Ruth Young (Cambridge: Cambridge University Press, 2015), 177–240, 216–24, esp. 219. The people of the Indus River Valley might also have acted as intermediaries in the trade of lapis-lazuli, which was imported from modern-day Afghanistan.

22   Crawford, *Ur*, 57.

23   Crawford, *Ur*, 57–8; C. Leonard Woolley, *Ur Excavations IV: The Early Periods* (Philadelphia: The American Philosophical Society, 1955), 35–6.

24   RIME 2.1.1.1 ll. 30–43.

25   RIME 2.1.2.3, ll. 1–29.

26   RIME 2.1.2.13.

27   RIME 2.1.3.1; Frayne, *Sargonic and Gutian Periods*, 74–5, 299.

28   Frayne, *Sargonic and Gutian Periods*, 74.

29   RIME 2.1.4.4.

30   RIME 2.1.4.5.

31   For Enlil's temple, see RIME 2.1.4.15 (Frayne, *Sargonic and Gutian Periods*, 184); for Nanna's, see RIME 2.1.4.17.

32   For example, Ashtar at Zabalam (RIME 2.1.4.16) and his own temple in Agade (RIME 2.1.4.10); see also Foster, *Age of Agade*, 14–6.

33   RIME 2.1.5.3.

34   Molina, 'Ur', 359.

35   RIME 3/1.1.6.12 and 13 (Edzard, *Gudea and His Dynasty*, 25–6).

36   E.g., Marc Van De Mieroop, 'Ur. A. II. Philologisch. Im frühen 2. Jahrtausend', *RlA* 14 (2014–2016): 361–4; Marc Van De Mieroop, 'Old Babylonian Ur: Portrait of an Ancient Mesopotamian City', *JANES* 21 (1992): 119–30. For the late second and first millennium BCE see John A. Brinkman, 'Ur. A. III. Philologisch. Mitte 2-1 Jahrtausend', *RlA* 14 (2014–2016): 364–7.

37   Hugo H. Figulla, 'Accounts Concerning Allocation of Provisions for Offerings in the Ningal-Temple at Ur', *Iraq* 15 (1953): 88–122; Marc Van De Mieroop, 'Sheep and Goat Herding According to the Old Babylonian Texts from Ur', *BSA* 7 (1993): 161–82; for the changes in the function of the Ganunmah, see Van De Mieroop, 'Old Babylonian Ur', 125.

38   Giacomo Di Giacomo e Giuseppe Scardozzi, 'Multitemporal High-Resolution Satellite Images for the Study and Monitoring of an Ancient Mesopotamian City and its Surrounding Landscape: The Case of Ur', *Geophys. J. Int.* 2012 (Article ID 716296), 1–14, esp. Figure 8a; C. Leonard Woolley, *Ur Excavations, Volume VI: The Buildings of the Third Dynasty of Ur* (London: The Trustees of the British Museum, 1974), 61–4.

39   In one of his royal inscriptions, Sargon boasts that he "moored the ships of Meluhha, Magan, and Dilmun at the quay of Agade" (RIME 2.1.1.11, ll. 9–13; translation slightly adapted after Frayne, *Sargonic and Gutian Periods*, 28).

40   Sally Dunham, 'Ancient Near Eastern Architecture', in *A Companion to the Ancient Near East*, ed. by Daniel C. Snell (Malden, MA: Blackwell Publishing, 2007), 289–303, 294.

41   While no archaeological remains of an Early Dynastic or Sargonic palace survive from Ur, documents confirm that one existed at least during the Early Dynastic period (Walther Sallaberger, 'Palast. A. I. Mesopotamien im III. Jahrtausend', *RlA* 10 (2004): 200–4, 201). For the Sargonic period, the extant documentation mentions palaces at Adab, Umma, Girsu, Isin, Susa, and Nippur, but not at Ur (Sallaberger, 'Palast', 202).

Enheduana the Priestess   75

42 Dunham, 'Ancient Near Eastern Architecture', 297.

43 Dunham, 'Ancient Near Eastern Architecture', 292.

44 Van De Mieroop, 'Ur', 362. Paolo Brusasco, 'Family Archives and Social Use of Space in Old Babylonian Houses at Ur', *Mesopotamia* XXXIV–XXXV (1999– 2000): 1–173, 145.

45 Peter A. Miglus, 'Prozession(sstrasse). B. Archäologisch', *RlA* 11 (2006): 103–5.

46 Marten P. Streck, 'Strasse (street, road). A. Philologisch', *RlA* 13 (2012): 206–8, 206; Peter A. Miglus, 'Strasse. B. Archäologisch', *RlA* 13 (2012): 208–10.

47 Heather D. Baker, 'A Waste of Space? Unbuilt Land in Babylonian Cities of the First Millennium BC', *Iraq* 71 (2009): 89–98, 94–5.

48 This was certainly the case during the Third Dynasty of Ur. Steve Tinney, 'Ur-Namma the Canal-Digger: Context, Continuity and Change in Sumerian Literature', *JCS* 51 (1999): 31–49.

49 For Sennacherib and its hanging garden, see Stephanie Dalley, *The Mystery of the Hanging Garden of Babylon. An Elusive World Wonder Traced* (Oxford, UK: Oxford University Press, 2013).

50 For the fourth–third millennium White Temple at Uruk, see Petr Charvát, *Mesopotamia Before History* (London: Routledge, 2002), 122; Guillermo Algaze, 'The End of Prehistory and the Uruk Period', in *The Sumerian World*, ed. by Harriet Crawford (New York: Routledge, 2013), 68–94, 76.

51 Beate Pongratz-Leisten, 'Mesopotamia', in *The Cambridge Companion to Ancient Mediterranean Religions*, ed. by Barbette Stanley Spaeth (Cambridge: Cambridge University Press, 2013), 33–54; Benjamin R. Foster, 'Mesopotamia', in *A Handbook of Ancient Religions*, ed. by John R. Hinnells (Cambridge: Cambridge University Press, 2009), 162–213; Jeremy Black and Andrew Green, *Gods, Demons and Symbols of Ancient Mesopotamia* (Austin: University of Texas Press, 1992).

52 Benjamin R. Foster, 'Akkadians', in *The Oxford Encyclopedia of the Ancient Near East*, ed. by Eric M. Meyers (New York/Oxford: Oxford University Press, 1997), 49–54.

53 Michael P. Streck, 'Eblaite and Old Akkadian', in *The Semitic Languages: An International Handbook*, ed. by Stefan Weniger (Berlin/Boston: De Gruyter, 2011), 340–59, 341.

54 An early study—Johannes J. van Dijk, 'Les contacts ethniques dans la Mésopotamie et les synchretismes de la religion sumérienne', Synchretism 3 (1969): 171–206, 188–91—suggests that Enheduana played a crucial role in this process. This view is, however, disputed by Foster, *Age of Agade*, 141–2, among others.

55 Brigitte Groneberg, 'Die sumerische-akkadische Inana/Ištar', *WO* 17 (1986): 25–46.

56 Foster, *Age of Agade*, 138. For the connection between Ashtar and Sargon's dynasty, see Rivkah Harris, 'Inanna/Ishtar as Paradox and a Coincidence of Opposites', *Hist. Rel.* 30, no. 3 (1991): 261–78, 271.

57 Manfred Krebernik, 'Mondgott. A. I. Philologisch', *RlA* 8 (1993–1998): 361–9; Foster, *Age of Agade*, 137.

58 Krebernik, 'Mondgott', 360–2. While Suen (written ^{d}**en-zu**) was an older form of the name attested during the third millennium BCE, Sin was in use from the Old Babylonian period onward. ^{d}**en-zu** is normalized as Suen in Sumerian personal names (e.g., Amar-Suen, "Calf of Sin") and as Sin in Akkadian ones (e.g., Namar-Sin, "Beloved of Sin").

59 Foster, *Age of Agade*, 137.

60 Benjamin R. Foster, 'Sumerian Mythology', in *The Sumerian World*, ed. by Harriet Crawford (London/New York: Routledge, 2013), 435–43.

76 *Enheduana*

61 Foster, 'Mesopotamia', 173–5.
62 Westenholz, 'The Old Akkadian Period', 78–84.
63 Foster, *Age of Agade*, 139.
64 Collon, *First Impressions*, 35.
65 Foster, *Age of Agade*, 141.
66 Nicole Brisch (ed.), *Religion and Power: Divine Kingship in the Ancient World and Beyond* (Chicago: University of Chicago Press, 2008); Gebhard J. Selz, "'The Holy Drum, the Spear, and the Harp." Towards an Understanding of the Problems of Deification in Third Millennium Mesopotamia', *Sumerian Gods and their Representations*, ed. by Irving L. Finkel and Markham J. Geller (Groningen: Styx Publications, 1997), 167–213.
67 Nicole Brisch, 'Of Gods and Kings: Divine Kingship in Ancient Mesopotamia', *Relig. Compass* 7, no. 2 (2013): 37–46.
68 Foster, *Age of Agade*, 141. Other examples include Marduk, poliad god of Babylon, in the second millennium, and Ashur, poliad god of Ashur, in the late second and first millennia.
69 Seth F. C. Richardson, 'On Seeing and Believing: Liver Divination and the Era of Warring States (II)', in *Divination and Interpretation of Signs in the Ancient World*, ed. by Amar Annus (Chicago, IL: The Oriental Institute of the University of Chicago, 2010), 225–66, 228–33.
70 Piotr Steinkeller, 'Appendix 1: The Priest-King in Uruk Times', in *History, Texts and Art in Early Babylonia: Three Essays*, by Piotr Steinkeller (Berlin/London: De Gruyter, 2017), 82–104. Steinkeller argues that the office was "a new development, whose purpose was to counterbalance the position of the en of Inana/ Uruk, and so to provide Sargon with an ideological and political base in southern Babylonia" (102).
71 The Sumerian terms referring to high priest(ess)es include **en**, **ereš-diŋir**, and **egi₂-zi**. Their Akkadian equivalents are *ēnum* and *ēntum*. While these terms are synonyms, geographical and diachronic differences are attested (Claudia Suter, 'Between Human and Divine: High Priestesses in Images from the Akkad to the Isin-Larsa Period', in *Ancient Near Eastern Art in Context: Studies in Honor of Irene J. Winter by Her Students*, ed. by Jack Cheng and Marion Feldman (Leiden/ Boston: Brill, 2007), 317–61, 318–9).
72 Selz, 'The Uruk Phenomenon', 216–8.
73 Suter, 'Between Human and Divine', 318, 321.
74 Irene J. Winter, 'Women in Public: The Disk of Enheduanna, the Beginning of the Office of En-Priestess and the Weight of Visual Evidence' in *La femme dans le proche orient antique*, ed. by Jean-Marie Durand (Paris: Éditions Recherche sur les Civilisations, 1987), 189–201. See also Annette Zgoll, *Des Rechtsfall der En-hedu-Ana in Lied nin-me-šara* (Münster: Ugarit-Verlag, 1997), 100.
75 Joan Goodnick Westenholz, 'En-Priestess: Pawn or Power Mogul?' in *Organization, Representation and Symbols of Power in the Ancient Near East*, ed. by Gernot Wilhelm (Winona Lake, IN: Eisenbrauns, 2012), 291–312, 297.
76 Joan Goodnick Westenholz, 'Enheduanna, En-Priestess, Hen of Nanna, Spouse of Nanna', in *DUMU-E2-DUB-BA-A. Studies in Honor of Åke W. Sjöberg*, ed. by Hermann Behrens, Darlene Loding and Martha T. Roth (Philadelphia: Occasional Publications of the Samuel Noah Kramer Fund, 1989), 539–56, 541. See also Westenholz, 'En-Priestess: Pawn or Power Mogul?', 300.
77 Westenholz, 'Enheduanna', 541.
78 Rhonda McHale-Moore, 'The Mystery of Enheduanna's Disk', *JANES* 27 (2000): 69–74.
79 Winter, 'Women in Public', 198–9.

Enheduana the Priestess 77

80 RIME 2.1.4.33.
81 Enmahgalana translates into "The majestic (and) great high priestess of the sky/ An."
82 Parsa Daneshmand, 'Extispicy and Consensus Decision-Making in Ancient Mesopotamia' *DABIR* 9, no. 1 (2022): 67–85.
83 Walther Sallaberger and Fabienne Huber Vulliet, 'Priester: A: I: Mesopotamien', *RlA* 10 (2003–2005): 617–40, 626–8.
84 Suter, 'Between Human and Divine', 318–9.
85 The only exception is the Akitu House, a religious structure erected outside of the city walls and used only in connection with the Akitu Festival. It housed the statue of a city's patron deity for a few days before its triumphant return to its main temple. However, the Akitu House was neither as large nor as elaborate as a temple. See Tammi J. Schneider, *An Introduction to Ancient Mesopotamian Religion* (Grand Rapids, IO: Wm. B. Eerdmans Publishing Co., 2011), 77–8.
86 Anne-Caroline Rendu-Loisel and Philippe Quenet, 'Introduction au temple: le bâtiment et ses hôtes', in *ana ziqquratim. Sur la piste de Babel*, ed. by Philippe Quenet (Strasbourg: Presses Universitaires de Strasbourg, 2016), 35–9, 35.
87 Suter, 'Between Human and Divine', 320.
88 Westenholz, 'En-Priestess: Pawn or Power Mogul?', 300.
89 Westenholz, 'Enheduanna', 547–8.
90 Jerrold S. Cooper, 'Sacred Marriage and Popular Cult in Early Mesopotamia', in *Official Cult and Popular Religion in the Ancient Near East*, ed. by Eiko Matsushima (Heidelberg: Universitätsverlag C. Winter, 1993), 81–96, 82.
91 The rulers for whom the sacred marriage ritual has been postulated practiced polygamy; Raymond Westbrook, 'Polygamie', *RlA* 10 (2003–2005): 600–2.
92 Cooper, 'Sacred Marriage', 82–3; Yitschak Sefati, *Love Songs in Sumerian Literature* (Bar-Ilan: Bar-Ilan University Press, 1998), 30–3; Johannes Renger, 'Heilige Hochzeit', *RlA* 4 (1972–1975): 251–9, and especially p. 257 for a critique of an early stage of the ritual.
93 Philip Jones, 'Embracing Inana: Legitimation and Mediation in the Ancient Mesopotamian Sacred Marriage Hymn *Iddin-Dagan A*', *JAOS* 123, no. 2 (2003): 291–302, 291; Pirjo Lapinkivi, 'The Sumerian Sacred Marriage and Its Aftermath', in *Sacred Marriages: The Divine-Human Sexual Metaphor from Sumer to Early Christianity*, ed. by Martti Nissinen and Risto Uro (Winona Lake, IN: Eisenbrauns, 2008), 7–42, 9–10.
94 For a diachronic overview of the rite, see Beate Pongratz-Leisten, 'Sacred Marriage and the Transfer of Divine Knowledge: Alliances between the Gods and the King in Ancient Mesopotamia', in *Sacred Marriages: The Divine-Human Sexual Metaphor from Sumer to Early Christianity*, ed. by Martti Nissinen and Risto Uro (Winona Lake, IN: Eisenbrauns, 2008), 43–73.
95 Westenholz, 'Enheduanna', 541–4.
96 Westenholz, 'En-Priestess: Pawn or Power Mogul?', 302.
97 Westenholz, 'En-Priestess: Pawn or Power Mogul?', 302.
98 *Inana B*, ll. 118–20.
99 For the meaning of the Sumerian term $gi_{(4)}$-**rin-na**, and attestation of Nanna's bed, see Westenholz, 'Enheduanna', 548.
100 Weadock, 'The *giparu* at Ur', 117–8, room C28 in Plate XXVI.
101 *Inana B*, ll. 67–8.
102 Jean Bottéro, *Religion in Ancient Mesopotamia*. Translated by Teresa Lavender Fagan (Chicago/London: University of Chicago Press, 2001), 128.
103 Bottéro, *Religion*, 131.
104 Eanedu was the last high priestess before the office fell into disuse (Madeline A. Fitzgerald, *The Rulers of Larsa* [Ph.D. diss., New Haven, Yale University,

78 Enheduana

2002], 134–5; Helle, *Enheduana*, 167–8). In her inscriptions, she referred to herself as **dumu** and **šeš** of kings. While **dumu** can be translated as "child" regardless of gender—although the term **dumu-munus**, "daughter," exists—**šeš** means "brother," not "sibling." For a possible explanation of this choice, see Brigitte Lion, 'Sexe et genre (2): Des prétesses fils de roi', *Topoi. Orient-Occident. Supplement 10* (2009): 185–92, 179.

105 RIME 4.2.14.20.
106 The term describing what had collapsed is lost in the break.
107 RIME 4.2.14.20, ll. 26–37, 40–3; translation slightly adapted after Douglas R. Frayne, *The Old Babylonian Period (2003–1595 BC)* (Toronto/Buffalo/London: The University of Toronto Press, 1990), 300.
108 Westenholz, 'Enheduanna', 546.
109 RIME 4.1.4.14. The legend reads, "A'aba, son of Enanatuma, high priestess of Nanna." Dominique Charpin, *Le clergé d'Ur au siècle d'Hammurabi* (XIXᵉ–XVIIIᵉ siècle av. J.-C.) (Paris-Genève: Librairie Droz, 1986), 218, prefers to translate the Sumerian term **dumu** as "servant" rather than "son."
110 Charpin, *Le clergé*, 195–210.
111 Charpin, *Le clergé d'Ur*, 215.
112 Sallaberger and Vulliet, 'Priester', 630.
113 See *Electronic Pennsylvania Sumerian Dictionary* at http://oracc.museum.upenn.edu/epsd2/sux, s.v. **gudu₄**.
114 For a recent discussion of the disk, see Helle, *Enheduana*, 113–9.
115 C. Leonard Woolley and Max Mallowan, *Ur Excavations Volume VII. The Old Babylonian Period* (London: The Trustees of the British Museum, 1974), 56; McHale-Moore, 'The Mystery of Enheduanna's Disk', 70.
116 Winter, 'Women in Public', 190.
117 Melanie J. Hatz, 'Disk of Enheduanna, Daughter of Sargon', in *Art of the First Cities. The Third Millennium B.C. from the Mediterranean to the Indus*, ed. by Joan Aruz with Ronald Wallenfels (New York/New Haven/London: The Metropolitan Museum of Art/Yale University Press, 2003), 200–1, no. 128, 211.
118 Violation of isocephaly is well attested in third millennium BCE Mesopotamian art, and it served to emphasize the primary role of the highest person (Winter, 'Women in Public', 193).
119 Johannes Renger, 'Untersuchungen zum Priestertum in der altbabylonischen Zeit', *ZA* 58 (1967): 110–88, 126, fn. 100.
120 Helle, *Enheduana*, 114.
121 RIME 2.1.1.16.
122 Winter, 'Women in Public', 192, fn. 17.
123 Contra Winter, 'Women in Public', 193.
124 Wilfred G. Lambert, 'The Pantheon of Mari', *Mari* 4 (1985): 525–39, 527; Helle, *Enheduana*, 113.
125 McHale-Moore, 'The Mystery of Enheduanna's Disk', 70.
126 RIME 4.1.4.13. The reference to Ningal's bedroom is intriguing. Unfortunately, it is difficult to establish not only the function of the room but also its location.
127 Weadock, 'The *giparu* at Ur', 108–9.
128 Helle, *Enheduana*, 117.
129 Weadock, 'The *giparu* at Ur', 108.
130 McHale-Moore, 'The Mystery of Enheduanna's Disk', 74.
131 *Sumerian King List*, ll. 224–7. For Kug-Bau see Sebastian Fink, 'Invisible Mesopotamian Royal Women?', in *The Routledge Companion to Women and Monarchy in the Ancient Mediterranean World*, ed. by Elizabeth D. Carney and Sabine Müller (New York: Routledge, 2021), 137–48, 141–2.

Enheduana the Priestess   79

132 Louis R. Siddall, *The Reign of Adad-nīrārī III: An Historical and Ideological Analysis of an Assyrian King and His Times* (Leiden: Brill, 2013), 86–100.

133 Eckart Frahm, 'From Sammu-ramat to Semiramis and Beyond: Metamorphoses of an Assyrian Queen', in *Women at the Dawn of History*, ed. by Agnete W. Lassen and Klaus Wagensonner (New Haven, CT: Yale Babylonian Collection, 2020), 46–53.

134 Selz, 'The Uruk Phenomenon', 216–8.

135 Marc Van de Mieroop, *The Ancient Mesopotamian City* (Oxford: Clarendon Press, 1997), 33–5.

136 RIME 1.9.3.5, col. i, ll. 2–9, col. ii, ll. 1–13, col. iii, ll. 4–6.

137 Westenholz, 'En-Priestess: Pawn or Power Mogul?', 301.

138 Zgoll, *Des Rechtsfall*, 99–107.

139 Westenholz, 'En-Priestess: Pawn or Power Mogul?', 301, 304.

140 Westenholz, 'En-Priestess: Pawn or Power Mogul?', 304.

141 Beate Pongratz-Leisten, 'Sanga', in *The Encyclopedia of Ancient History*, ed. by Roger S. Bagnall et al. (New York: Blackwell Publishing Ltd, 2013), 6033–4; Sallaberger and Vulliet, 'Priester', 628–9.

142 See *Electronic Pennsylvania Sumerian Dictionary* at http://oracc.museum.upenn .edu/epsd2/sux, s.v. **saŋŋa**.

143 Charpin, *Le clergé d'Ur*, 214–5.

144 *Electronic Pennsylvania Sumerian Dictionary* at http://oracc.museum.upenn.edu /epsd2/sux, s.v. **šita**.

145 UET 5, 343 (P415225). The tablet dates to Rim-Sin's 30th regnal year and was unearthed at Ur.

146 For Nippur, see Elizabeth Stone, 'The Social Role of the *nadītu* Women in Old Babylonian Nippur', *JESHO* 25 (1982): 50–70; for Sippar, see Sara Lahtinen, *The nadītum as a Businesswoman. Economic Enterprise Among Religiously Devoted Women in Old Babylonian Sippar* (Saarbrücken: Lambert Academic Publishing, 2011) and Katrien De Graef, '*Cherchez la femme!* The Economic Role of Women in Old Babylonian Sippar', in *The Role of Women in Work and Society in the Ancient Near East*, ed. by Brigitte Lion and Cécile Michel (Berlin/Boston: De Gruyter, 2016), 270–95.

147 Schrakamp, 'A View from Within', 650–3.

148 Schrakamp, 'A View from Within', 650–1.

149 Schrakamp, 'A View from Within', 651.

150 Westenholz, 'The Old Akkadian Period', 61–2.

151 http://oracc.museum.upenn.edu/epsd2/sux, s.v. (Sumerian); CAD G, s.v. 83–4 (Akkadian).

152 Weadock, 'The *giparu* at Ur'; Charpin, *Le clergé d'Ur*, 192–220

153 Crawford, *Ur*, 76–9.

154 Weadock, 'The *giparu* at Ur', 105. Weadock, 'The *giparu* at Ur', 106, does not rule out the possibility of earlier buildings since archaeological levels before the Early Dynastic period were not investigated.

155 This is corroborated by inscriptions by Ur-Namma (e.g., RIME 3/2.1.1.2 and 3/2.1.1.11) and Amar-Suen (RIME 3/2.1.3.7). Amar-Suen also built (or more likely rebuilt or refurbished) the **ŋipar** itself (e.g., RIME 3/2.1.3.8)

156 Crawford, *Ur*, 90.

157 Charpin, *Le clergé d'Ur*, 193–4.

158 Crawford, *Ur*, 91.

159 Federico Zaina, *The Urban Archaeology of Early Kish. 3rd Millennium BCE Levels At Tell Ingharra* (Bologna: Ante Quem S.r.l. 2020), 142; J. Nicholas Postgate, 'Early Dynastic Burial Customs at Abu Salabikh', *Sumer* 36 (1980):

80 Enheduana

     65–82; Caroline S. Steele, *Living with the Dead: House Burials at Abu Salabikh, Iraq* (Ph.D. diss., The State University of New York at Binghamton, Binghamton, 1990).

160 Crawford, *Ur*, 91.

161 Weadock, 'The *giparu* at Ur', 109–11.

162 Crawford, *Ur*, 92.

163 Room C28. Weadock, 'The *giparu* at Ur', 117–8.

164 Room C27. The layout made it possible for the statue to be visible to everyone accessing the temple from its southeastern entrance. This person would cross three antechambers (C1, C2, and C3), and then turn to enter the main courtyard (C7) from room C3. Already from this position, the statue would be visible straight ahead.

165 Charpin, *Le clergé d'Ur*, 195.

166 Woolley and Mallowan, *Ur Excavations, Volume VII*, 55–6.

167 Charpin, *Le clergé d'Ur*, 195–216.

168 Charpin, *Le clergé d'Ur*, 215 and 218.

169 *Electronic Pennsylvania Sumerian Dictionary* at http://oracc.museum.upenn .edu/epsd2/sux, s.v. **kinda** lists only five occurrences, and in two cases the term is clearly not to be interpreted as a profession but as a designation for a type of textile. Hair was an important marker of status in the region not just during the Sargonic period. Sargonic men, too, might have used coiffeurs (Max E. L. Mallowan, 'The Bronze Head of the Akkadian Period from Nineveh', *Iraq* 3, no. 1 (1936): 104–10). Indeed, a Sargonic royal hairstyle has been identified (Nigro, 'The Two Steles of Sargon', 94 and fn. 22).

170 Helle, *Enheduana*, 109–10.

171 *Electronic Pennsylvania Sumerian Dictionary* at http://oracc.museum.upenn.edu /epsd2/sux, s.v. **šabra**.

172 Mark E. Cohen, *Festivals and Calendars of the Ancient Near East* (Bethesda, MD: CDL Press, 2015), 135–9. During the third millennium BCE, two festivals of the dead are attested: one took place during the month of **ne-izi-ŋar** (July/ August) and took its name from the month itself. A similar festival occurred during the month of **ab(a)-e₃** (December/January), also named after the month. From the late third millennium BCE onwards, another festival was introduced in the calendar, **a-bu-um**. It might have had Amorite origins, and its relationship and difference with the pre-existing festivals of the dead are unclear. This term came to identify the fifth month of the year (July/August) and so paralleled **ne-izi-ŋar**.

173 For instance, rooms A11–23 had religious functions. Specifically, A14 and A16 were antecellas, while A18 was a shrine with an altar and bases for cultic statues.

174 Giorgio Buccellati, 'Through a Tablet Darkly: A reconstruction of Old Akkadian Monuments described in Old Babylonian Copies', in *The Tablet and the Scroll: Near Eastern Studies in Honor of William W. Hallo*, ed. by Mark E. Cohen, Daniel Snell and David B. Weisberg (Bethesda, MD: CDL Press, 1993), 58–71; Schrakamp, 'A View from Within', 627.

175 Schrakamp, 'A View from Within', 627; Ingo Schrakamp, 'Militär und Kriegführung in Vorderasien', in *Krieg: eine archäologische Spurensuch*, ed. by Harald Meller and Michael Schefzik (Darmstadt: Landesamt für Denkmalpflege und Archäologie, 2016), 213–24, 216.

176 Schrakamp, 'A View from Within', 635–8; Foster, *Age of Agade*, 40–1.

177 Schrakamp, 'A View from Within', 637–8.

178 For the names of some of these festivals, see Cohen, *Festivals and Calendars*, 72–4. For the calendar of the city of Ur during the third millennium BCE, see Cohen, *Festivals and Calendars*, 71–113.

Enheduana the Priestess 81

179 Cohen, *Festivals and Calendars*, 100–1.
180 Andrew R. George, *House Most High. The Temples of Ancient Mesopotamia* (Winona Lake, IN: Eisenbrauns, 1993), 114.
181 Adab 085+840 (P217542) (Cohen, *Festivals and Calendars*, 100).

5   Enheduana the Poetess

Introduction

Is Enheduana truly the first documented author in world history? Did she write the hymns where she speaks in the first person—**nin me šar₂-ra**, "Queen of all Cosmic Powers" (*Inana B*), and **in-nin ša₃ gur₄-ra**, "Great-hearted Mistress" (*Inana C*)?[1] If so, then what about **in-nin me huš-a**, "Mistress of the Fearsome Cosmic Powers" (*Inana and Ebih*), which echoes some of the themes and the tone of *Inana B* and *Inana C* but makes no mention of Enheduana?[2] Did Enheduana contribute to the *Temple Hymns*, for which she is credited as the compiler?[3] What about *Nanna C*, the hymn in celebration of Nanna's temple, or *Nanna B*, a dialogue between Nanna and Ningal with erotic undertones?[4] Did she speak in the third person in the only literary tablet from the third millennium BCE preserving her name, but admittedly too broken to fully understand?[5] If so, why did she use the third person, a switch that also occurs at the end of *Inana B*?[6] Was this a form of self-representation?[7] Or something else altogether?

If the answer to any of these questions is an unequivocal "yes," then the earliest recorded author in world history was a woman. And not just any woman, but a princess and a priestess working in concert with her family to further its political ambitions. Through hymns celebrating Nanna, the deity whom she served daily, as well as Inana/Ashtar, the goddess who protected her family and their city, Agade, she contributed to furthering the Sargonic agenda while also asserting her own voice.

Yet, an unequivocal "yes" is hard to come by because the question of Enheduana's authorship is complicated. To untangle it, several elements need to be considered. First, a review of the previous scholarship aids in understanding the topic's complexities. Second, examining Mesopotamian emic categories of genre emphasizes the pitfalls of using modern labels to classify ancient texts. Third, Mesopotamian conceptions of authorship must be addressed since the notion of Enheduana's authorship did not exist in a vacuum. Finally, our corpus of seven texts must be scrutinized—not just thematically and interpretatively but also in the context in which it was copied and studied: early second millennium BCE scribal education, with a keen eye to the role that traditional characters played therein.

DOI: 10.4324/9781032641164-5

Enheduana the Poetess   83

I submit that the works attributed to Enheduana are not hers, in the same vein that the heroic deeds attributed to Sargon and Naram-Sin in later pseudo-historical traditions are not theirs—although they were based on the awareness of these rulers' successes. Rather, later scribes and scholars ascribed to Enheduana works composed, at the earliest, during the Third Dynasty of Ur. Yet, this process would only have been possible if Enheduana was indeed a renowned author. As such, she was uniquely positioned to become a traditional character to whom magnificent compositions could be attributed. What she wrote, however, is not what survives.

A (Very) Brief History of the Scholarship

There is no scholarly consensus regarding Enheduana's authorship. Some accept it unequivocally—at times even uncritically. Others argue that she was not an author at all. Others yet seek a more nuanced approach to advance our understanding of Mesopotamian authorship.

Scholars who argue that Enheduana authored *Inana B*, *Inana C*, the *Temple Hymns*, *Nanna C*, and the composition preserved on a fragmentary late third-millennium tablet do so primarily because Enheduana is seemingly mentioned in the text. Statements vary, but on occasion, Enheduana's role as an author is accepted without any attempt at problematizing the matter.[8] To be sure, the primary concern of earlier generations of scholars was to make these compositions accessible by publishing editions and translations. The topic of authorship was not a focus of research. Furthermore, the initial discovery by modern scholars of an ancient named author, and a woman at that, was hailed as a major achievement in a literary production that was largely anonymous.[9] Challenging the truthfulness of statements made in ancient texts might have seemed counterproductive.

Enheduana's authorship has been championed also by scholars who privilege a documentary approach, wherein literary compositions are used as sources to reconstruct historical events.[10] This view has been criticized, however, as ancient scribes had more suitable genres available to convey historical information and used them precisely for this purpose.[11]

Conversely, scholars who argue against Enheduana's authorship do so primarily because of the lack of Sargonic period manuscripts preserving the literary works in which her name appears.[12] Most of the tablets of the above-mentioned compositions were written during the nineteenth and eighteenth centuries BCE, long after Enheduana's death. Furthermore, at least in one case (*Inana C*), analysis of the language and lexicon suggests a Larsa Dynasty compositional date (c. 1924–1763 BCE).[13]

Also problematic is that Enheduana's most renowned compositions elevated the goddess Inana and not Nanna, whom she served as high priestess. On the one hand, this obstacle can be overcome since Inana's Akkadian counterpart, Ashtar, was the tutelary deity of Agade and the Sargonic royal family.

84   *Enheduana*

On the other hand, one wonders why, especially in *Inana B*, Inana's elevation occurred at Nanna's expense. Relatedly, if the purpose of such texts was to elevate Agade's tutelary deity, one wonders why her name was Inana rather than Ashtar, and why such elevation was conveyed in Sumerian only, even in occupied Ur.[14]

As such, some scholars have opted to separate the historical Enheduana from the author of the compositions attributed to her.[15] In this context, the question of Enheduana's authorship appears to be an Old Babylonian matter.[16] Moreover, attention has been paid to the overall anonymity of Sumerian literature to highlight that Enheduana and others "were authors only in a partial sense. Lost in a sea of anonymous literary creation, their names simply became words in a text."[17]

In more recent years, scholars have used innovative approaches to examine Enheduana's contributions to the history of literature. For instance, it has been suggested that Enheduana's role be better understood through the metaphor of weaving, borrowed from Kashmiri studies.[18] Through this lens, "[a]uthorship was thought of as weaving old threads into new textiles: the material being reshaped may have had a long history, but the poet would arrange it according to an individual design, and therein lay the author's contribution."[19]

Alternatively, three Enheduanas have been identified: a real person who lived during much of the twenty-fourth century BCE; "a figure of prominence in Sumerian literature of the Old Babylonian Period"; and an "icon of poetry and authorship" who became popular in the last quarter of the twentieth century CE in the aftermath of second wave feminism.[20] This differentiation does not diminish Enheduana's contributions. Specifically, it mattered "to the Old Babylonian scholars and scribes that her authorship be prominently displayed, and moreover, that this same authorship appear[ed] in connection with her three major works.[21]

Such a view is not isolated. Enheduana has been deemed an example of attributed authorship because of her role as a cultural hero.[22] Within this framework, Enheduana was "a suitable counterpart of Nisaba," the Sumerian goddess of writing and the scribal arts. In particular, she resonated among Old Babylonian priests responsible for literary production since she was a priestess who, like them, was an author. Furthermore, "[a]s a historical figure, she was a proper anchor in time and space."[23] In other words, Enheduana's authority derived from her own historicity.

While brief, this survey shows that the matter of Enheduana's authorship has not been settled. I suspect that it might never be unless new documents come to light. Meanwhile, I put forward a different approach by using new angles, namely the question of Mesopotamian genre, authorship, the Old Babylonian scribal curriculum, and the role of traditional characters in cuneiform literature. Let us begin with a consideration of genre.

On Mesopotamian Genre

No known cuneiform texts elucidate the Mesopotamian discourse on literary genres.[24] To be sure, native terms have been identified, for example in, doxologies and colophons—short notations at the end of a composition or tablet. Nevertheless, modern scholars shy away from an emic approach to the study of Mesopotamian genre categories, that is the classification of Mesopotamian compositions by using Sumerian or Akkadian terminology. Rather, an etic approach is preferred: these texts are designated by using terms such as myth, epic, song, love poetry, or wisdom literature, which derive from biblical and classical scholarship and have been useful in the cross-disciplinary study of Mesopotamian literature.[25] However, they create differences between ancient compositions where none existed.

Three of the compositions attributed to Enheduana provide a relevant example: *Inana B*, *Inana C*, and *Inana and Ebih*. In Sumerian, these texts end with the so-called za_2-mi_3 formula, "Praise to (a deity)" (in these cases: "Praise to Inana"). This formula is widely attested in the Old Babylonian period but rarely found outside of curricular compositions.[26] In modern parlance, *Inana B* and *Inana C* have been classified as hymns, and *Inana and Ebih* as a myth. This categorization introduces a false dichotomy and obscures the striking similarities among the three compositions, which were recognized also in antiquity.[27] Incidentally, every hymn preserved in the *Temple Hymns* also concludes with the za_2-mi_3 formula—the deity praised is the patron god or goddess of the temple being celebrated.

Sumerian labels tended to focus on performance, as is the case for **adab** or **tigi** songs.[28] The former designated a drum, while the latter might have been a drum or another percussion instrument.[29] **šir₃-gid₂-da** means "extended song"; **bal-bal-e** indicates a composition performed as a back and forth by two different persons or groups, singing in turn. Only one of these labels applies to our small corpus: *Nanna B* and *Nanna C* are **bal-bal-e**, a label also used for non-curricular texts.

Using an emic approach to the study of the compositions attributed to Enheduana situates most of them (*Inana B*, *Inana C*, *Inana and Ebih*, and the *Temple Hymns*) within the curricular setting of the Old Babylonian period by the presence of the za_2-mi_3 formula. The implications of this conclusion will be discussed further below. Meanwhile, it is time to examine Mesopotamian authorship more closely.

Authorship in Cuneiform Literature

The study of Mesopotamian authorship is complicated by three primary obstacles: (1) the scarcity of named authors; (2) the uncertainty in identifying the original text; and (3) the limited scope of research thus far.

86 *Enheduana*

First, most Mesopotamian literature was anonymous.[30] In more than 3,000 years of documented history, only a handful of authors can be identified by name.[31] Additionally, almost no authors are attested in documents dating to the time when they allegedly lived. Typically, they are credited with authorship by later scholars, their names preserved on copies of their works dating centuries after their lifetime, as in Enheduana's case.

Second, we face difficulties in reconstructing the original text, as we rarely possess autographed manuscripts. As such, the best we can hope for is to identify an archetype manuscript—the version of a text that is chronologically closest to the original one.[32] Relatedly, the circumstances in which most Mesopotamian compositions originated are lost to us. Likely, many existed first in an oral form and were not intended to be experienced through writing—many were never written down. Others might have been conceived originally as written compositions, as was the case for some Old Babylonian school texts.

Moreover, Mesopotamian literature was copied by students and professional scribes century after century. This process inevitably led to changes because of the unintended variants caused by a copyist's mistake or misunderstanding.[33] Some ancient scholars also enacted deliberate textual editing.[34] This was viewed as enriching and updating the text to suit the needs and attitudes of the current community of students and scholars.[35] Thereby, ancient authors used and reused compositions, thus maintaining the work's authority while also adding prestige to themselves. Plagiarism was something to be embraced, not avoided.[36]

Third, modern approaches to the study of ancient authors have been narrow in scope, typically lumping ancient authors into two main categories: the conveyors who claimed to have received their work from the gods, a common trope in world literature;[37] and the copyists who ensured the transmission of the texts but had nothing to do with their creation.[38] Neither approach allows ancient authors much agency. Recent studies have tried to rectify this, for example by introducing two new categories: instrumental and independent agency.[39] Instrumental agency is seen in those who transmitted literary works by copying them faithfully—their agency limited by their role. Independent agency refers to the creation of new compositions and the deliberate editing of old ones.

Despite these obstacles, there is evidence for authorship in Mesopotamian sources. The only ancient accounting of authors comes from the first millennium BCE *Catalogue of Texts and Authors* (ancient title: *āšipūtu* : *kalûtu* : **ud an ᵈen-lil₂**, "The Exorcists' Lore : The Lamentation Priests' Lore : 'When Anu and Enlil'"). It attributes literary compositions and omen collections to specific individuals.[40] Some of them are mythical characters such as Enmerkar (a king of Uruk who invented cuneiform) and Adapa (a king of Kish who inadvertently lost the immortality he'd been offered).[41] Most of the individuals mentioned by the *Catalogue* might have existed, however.

Enheduana the Poetess   87

The *Catalogue* was likely an attempt by eighth- and seventh-century Assyrian scribes "to make sense of a new cultural reality" at a time when Aramaic had begun to replace Akkadian as the primary spoken language.[42] Therefore, this text was less concerned with authorship and more with "establish[ing] an order of authority" among various documents, many of which were already exceedingly old.[43]

Aside from the attributions of authorship in the *Catalogue of Texts and Authors*, there are three authorship scenarios in Mesopotamia.[44] First, a tablet might be signed with the name of the scribe that copied it—a form of instrumental agency. Numerous examples survive, although for the most part, these signatures are found in copies of scholarly documents and not literary ones.[45]

Second, first-person narratives were assigned retroactively to historical characters. These pseudo-epigraphic texts are also called "fictional autobiographies" by modern scholars. An excellent example is the autobiographies of Sargon.[46] While the Old Babylonian version is badly damaged, the Neo-Assyrian *Sargon Birth Legend* is better preserved.[47] In both, Sargon speaks in the first person, thereby providing the illusion that he dictated, possibly even authored, the written text. The extent to which the people who accessed these compositions believed that the narrator and the author were one and the same is unclear.[48]

Third, literary works written in the third person could be attributed to specific individuals, and that attribution became canonical—the person's name forever associated with a creative act, which nobody dared question. Pseudo-epigraphic texts and third-person narratives are forms of attributed authorship, wherein authorship was allocated either by the initial author or compiler or by a later editor.[49] A few such cases are worth discussing.

Eighth- and seventh-century Assyrian scholars ascribed to one Sin-leqi-unnini authorship of the Standard Babylonian Version of the *Epic of Gilgamesh*.[50] Not much else is known about Sin-leqi-unnini, except that the *Catalogue of Texts and Authors* lists the epic as the work of Sin-leqi-unnini, the exorcist.[51] In addition, "many cult-singers (...) and intellectuals of the priestly classes of Late Babylonian Uruk considered [Sin-leqi-unnini] their remote ancestor."[52] Yet, even if the name Sin-leqi-unnini is attested as early as the Old Babylonian period, and so are Akkadian manuscripts preserving Gilgamesh's stories, there is no evidence that such a person ever existed.[53] As such, he might very well have been a (real or mythical) poet to whom later scholars attributed the composition of the *Epic of Gilgamesh*. Alternatively, Sin-leqi-unnini was a late second millennium scholar who "establish[ed] the Epic of Gilgamesh in the form familiar from first-millennium copies."[54]

A second case study is that of Bullussa-rabi, associated with the composition of a first-millennium hymn to Gula, the Mesopotamian goddess of healing.[55] The final lines of this hymn read:

88   *Enheduana*

> O Gula, great lady, whose help is Ninurta.
> Intercede for her with the mighty one,
> Your splendid spouse
> That he bring forth recovery for Bullussa-rabi,
> That the latter may kneel before you daily.[56]

The *Catalogue of Texts and Authors* goes further by attributing authorship to Bullussa-rabi of not just this hymn but three other Akkadian compositions yet to be identified.[57] It also informs us that Bullussa-rabi was "the exorcist, scholar of Babylon."[58] Notably, Bullussa-rabi was a woman.[59] Her name means "Her (that is Gula's) healing is great." The name's popularity during the late Kassite period (c. 1595–1155 BCE) indicates that she might have lived during the thirteenth century BCE.[60] Yet, no documents from this—or any other period—survive attesting to her historicity.

A final example is that of Kabti-ilani-Marduk, who claimed authorship of *Erra and Ishum*, also known as the *Epic of Erra* or the *Erra Poem*. *Erra and Ishum* is an Akkadian myth describing the havoc that the god of pestilence Erra (identified with Nergal) wreaked among the people. Erra's anger, awakened by agents of chaos, was eventually appeased by his counselor Ishum so that the rest of humankind was spared.[61] A section towards the end of the composition reads:

> The compiler of [this] text was Kabti-ilāni-Marduk, son of Dābibu: he (Ishum) revealed it to him in a nocturnal vision and, just as he (the poet) declaimed it while wakeful, so he left nothing out, he added to it not a single line.[62]

The poem continues by providing a justification for its existence. By means of *Erra and Ishum*, "Kabti-ilani-Marduk wants [to] open the eyes of people—everywhere and at all times—to Erra as the most violent power in the world, that is to the terrible reality of war."[63] In the absence of contemporary documents attesting to Kabti-ilani-Marduk's existence, we cannot deduce his reasonings and the historical events that might have prompted the inception of the poem. Nevertheless, this attribution might have been preserved also in the first millennium BCE *Catalogue of Texts and Authors*, which states that *Erra and Ishum* was "revealed" to someone, whose name is lost in a break.[64]

The case of Kabti-ilani-Marduk is remarkable because the true author is ostensibly divine—Ishum, Erra's advisor, shared the tale so that it would be known among the people. And Kabti-ilani-Marduk followed Ishum's text to the letter (or the wedge as the case may be).[65] Thus, Kabti-ilani-Marduk was celebrated not as the creator but as the human compiler (Akkadian *kāṣir kammēšu,* 'its compiler').[66] This was also how Enheduana was remembered in relation to the *Temple Hymns*, as we shall see.

Enheduana the Poetess 89

Additional cases are attested, but these examples suffice to illustrate the complexities of Mesopotamian authorship. Noteworthy is the fact that retroactively attributing works to earlier mythical and historical characters was a common practice. Whether Enheduana was the first individual for whom this process occurred is impossible to determine. At present, she is the earliest attested one. Let us now consider the compositions that made her famous.

The Compositions Attributed to Enheduana: Context, Summary, Analysis

As already discussed (Chapter 1), more compositions have been attributed to Enheduana than contemporary documents preserving her name. They celebrate deities or temples and so align well with Enheduana's role as high priestess. While the thematic similarities of some of these compositions are obvious, and will be discussed later in this chapter, this overview groups them as follows: (1) the compositions where the sign sequence **en-he₂-du₇-an-na** is unequivocally rendered as Enheduana, the name of Sargon's daughter (*Inana B*, *Inana C*, and the *Temple Hymns*); (2) the compositions where the sign sequence **en-he₂-du₇-an-na** may be rendered either as Enheduana or as **en he₂-du₇ an-na**, "lord, the ornament of the sky" (*Nanna C* and the third-millennium text); and (3) the compositions where the sign sequence **en-he₂-du₇-an-na** does not appear (*Nanna B* and *Inana and Ebih*). This approach will allow us to narrow down the corpus of Enheduana-related texts.

Inana B is attested on around 100 Old Babylonian tablets.[67] The majority was discovered in Nippur, where the hymn was part of the scribal curriculum. Some were unearthed in Ur, and a few are unprovenanced. At its core, *Inana B* is a grandiose celebration of Inana as the supreme deity of the Mesopotamian pantheon.[68] This is achieved through a very elaborate structure and the use of sophisticated poetic devices. The hymn opens with a description of Inana's powers (ll. 1–65). These are the same divine powers Inana stole from Enki, as we learn from another Old Babylonian Sumerian composition, *Inana and Enki*, whose curricular function is unclear.[69] Oblique references to other myths, about which we know next to nothing, permeate this introduction (as they do *Inana C*). *Inana B* is therefore in constant dialog with other compositions—more than survived to the vagaries of time. The hymnic introduction also underscores Inana's status as Nanna/Sin's "eldest daughter."[70]

The glorification of Inana is also achieved by using Enheduana's life experience as a plot device (ll. 66–143). In this section, Nanna's inaction at Enheduana's plight is deftly juxtaposed to Inana's willingness to intervene:

Let it be known, indeed, let it be known that Nanna said nothing, that he said, "It is up to you!"

90 *Enheduana*

Let it be known that you (Inana) are as lofty as the skies.
Let it be known that you are as vast as the earth.
Let it be known that you destroy rebel lands.
Let it be known that you roar at the foreign lands.
Let it be known that you kill.
Let it be known that you devour corpses like a dog. ...
Nanna said nothing, he (simply) said, "It is up to you!"[71]

Nanna's silence reflects the popular motif of divine abandonment to explain why a city, or a people, experiences hardship. In other words, it is Nanna's presumed abandonment of Ur that enabled Lugal-Ane's rebellion and Enheduana's subsequent exile. The final section (ll. 144–154) depicts Inana's intervention. As the hymn switches from first to third person, Enheduana's return to her residence is celebrated, alongside the goddess Inana. Highly lyrical and emotionally charged, *Inana B* is considered the most historical among the works attributed to Enheduana, as it refers to the Great Revolt by mentioning one of the rebel leaders known from earlier literary traditions: Lugal-Ane of Uruk.

Equally lyrical but not as obviously autobiographical is *Inana C*. It, too, survives exclusively on Old Babylonian tablets, about 35, mostly from Nippur. Others come from Shaduppum (mod. Tell 'Abu Harmal), one was found at Sippar-Yahrurum (mod. Tell Abu Habbah), and at least one was uncovered at Susa.[72] *Inana C* is unique among the compositions attributed to Enheduana because some exemplars contain an interlinear Old Babylonian (*not* Old Akkadian) translation. One of these comes from Nippur while the rest were unearthed at Shaduppum, but their precise archaeological context is unclear.[73] Presumably, these were school exercises, and part of the assignment was to translate the Sumerian text into Akkadian.

Like *Inana B*, *Inana C* extols Inana's powers, elevating her above all gods. The hymn opens with an overview of Inana's mythical biography, highlighting her main achievements, some of which are known from other sources (ll. 1–114). Emphasis is placed on Inana's martial powers and the violence that follows her. Other attributes are enumerated, some of them contradictory (ll. 115–218):

To destroy and to create, to remove and to settle are yours, Inana.
To turn men into women, to turn women into men are yours, Inana. ...
Profit and gain, financial loss and deficit are yours, Inana. ...
To neglect and to care, to arise and bow down are yours, Inana.[74]

It is due to these contradictions that "[m]ore strongly than any other poem from the ancient Near East, [*Inana C*] brings out the power and paradoxical nature of

Enheduana the Poetess 91

Inana."[75] Inana's complex character presented a challenge for other deities—
her conflicts with her relatives are well documented.[76] Nevertheless, these
powers contribute to her elevation—a motif that *Inana C* shares with *Inana B*.
Enheduana appears towards the end of the composition (ll. 219–242),
where she speaks in the first person, although most of what she says is lost
in a break:

> I am Enheduana, the hen (of Nanna).
> I am [Enheduana, the spouse] of Nanna.
> (approximately 20 lines missing)
> I am yours! This shall always be so. May your heart be kind towards
> me.
> (…)
> My own body experienced your great punishment.
> Lament and evil keep me awake; pain *splits me apart*.
> Mercy, compassion, care, lenience, and grace are yours,
> And so are drowning storms, opening lands and darkness turning into
> light.[77]

It is unclear whether Enheduana's plight was a plot device to exalt Inana, as in
Inana B. It is certain, however, that *Inana C* presents a view of Mesopotamian
mythological underpinnings that differs significantly from later third- and
early second-millennium-BCE compositions. Here, Inana is depicted as the
head of the pantheon: "the great gods kissed the earth and prostrated themselves (before her)."[78] The hymn goes as far as to claim that, "Without Inana,
great An can make no decisions, Enlil can allocate no destinies."[79] The final
stanzas (ll. 254–274) also celebrate Inana's powers and exhort that Inana's
heart "be restored for my (that is Enheduana's) sake."[80]

The *Temple Hymns* is a collection of 42 hymns to various temples.[81]
Especially popular in Nippur during the Old Babylonian period (almost 40
manuscripts have been uncovered there), the *Temple Hymns* is also attested
in Ur.[82] One manuscript dates to the Third Dynasty of Ur, which might have
been the milieu in which the hymns were assembled in their current form.[83]
Yet, the compositional history of the *Temple Hymns* was noteworthy already
in antiquity, as evidenced by the following statement, located at the end of
the text:

> The **lu₂ zu₂ keše₂-da** of the tablet was Enheduana.
> My king! Something has been born which had not been born before.[84]

The literal translation of this expression is "the one who puts together knowledge." Most commentators, however, have typically rendered this Sumerian

92   Enheduana

expression as "compiler." Yet, it has been argued recently that "weaver" is a better translation. Through this lens, "[t]he material being reshaped may have had a long history, but the poet would arrange it according to an individual design, and therein lay the author's contribution."[85] Needless to say, the Sumerian text does not suggest that Enheduana was the originator, author, or composer of these hymns.

Thematically, the *Temple Hymns* opens with a hymn to the Eabzu, the sanctuary of Enki in Eridu, and, incidentally, the oldest archaeologically documented temple structure.[86] Main sanctuaries such as those of Enlil in Nippur, Ningirsu in Lagash, Inana in Uruk, Nergal in Kutha, and Utu at Larsa and Sippar are also celebrated, encompassing all the main Mesopotamian cultic centers. The significance of this will be discussed later in this chapter. Suffice it to say here that this was done deliberately.

The compositions where the sign sequence **en-he$_2$-du$_7$-an-na** occurs, but most likely does not indicate Enheduana, are a fragmentary text dated to the third millennium BCE and *Nanna C*. The former was uncovered at Nippur. Since its first line does not survive, we do not know its ancient title, nor has a modern one been ascribed to it, as too little remains of the text.[87] Mention is made of Nanna, his temple, and the **en me-kug-kug-ge-eš$_3$ pa$_3$-da en he$_2$-du$_7$ an-na**.[88] These two lines have been translated as, "the high priestess chosen for her pure divine powers, Enheduana."[89] Alternatively, they have been rendered as, "the lord chosen for his pure divine powers, the lord, ornament of the sky," an epithet for the moon god Nanna himself.[90] Considering that "divine powers" (Sumerian **me**) are restricted to deities, the latter translation is more likely.[91]

Nanna C is preserved only on one Old Babylonian tablet from Nippur, which contains four **bal-bal-e** to Nanna.[92] *Nanna C* is the only one in which the sign sequence **en-he$_2$-du$_7$-an-na** appears. This composition celebrates the main temple of Nanna in Ur, the "House of Alabaster." It also mentions the **e$_2$-temen-ni$_2$-guru$_3$**, "House whose Foundation is Clad in Awe," the name of the ziggurat terrace from the Third Dynasty of Ur onwards.[93] That this moniker had been chosen by Ur-Namma, the founder of the dynasty, is confirmed by an inscription preserved on foundation cones uncovered in the ziggurat and surrounding areas.[94] Thus, the name of the ziggurat terrace indicates that the composition *cannot* predate the Third Dynasty of Ur. As such, the sign sequence **en he$_2$-du$_7$ an-na** is likely an epithet for Nanna.[95]

In conclusion, these two compositions were likely originally composed during the Third Dynasty of Ur as part of the elevation of Nanna when his city, Ur, became the capital of a large territorial state. Enheduana is not attested in either. Rather, the sign sequence is an epithet for Nanna, and a very suitable one at that: as the most brilliant among the night sky's celestial bodies, he was indeed the "lord, ornament of the sky."

Nanna B is the first composition in which the sign sequence **en-he$_2$-du$_7$-an-na** does not appear, even if Enheduana's authorship has been suggested.[96]

Enheduana the Poetess 93

Attested in the same Old Babylonian tablet from Nippur containing *Nanna C*, *Nanna B*, too, is a **bal-bal-e** to Nanna, specifically a love dialogue between Nanna and Ningal.[97] There is no evidence for Enheduana's involvement. Contextually, the mention of a *zirru* of Nanna must be read as an epithet of Ningal, who is the divine hen of Nanna, and not as a reference to her earthly counterpart.[98]

Inana and Ebih is the second composition in which the sign sequence **en-he₂-du₇-an-na** does not appear, even if Enheduana's authorship has been posited for it.[99] Attested on around 80 Old Babylonian manuscripts, this story was popular at Nippur and Ur; a few sources come from Sippar and Susa, while others are unprovenanced.[100] *Inana and Ebih* highlights Inana's martial nature and focuses on the war between Inana and Ebih, a minor deity possibly identified with Mount Hamrin who refused to bow before Inana.[101] The story opens with a celebration of Inana's might (ll. 1–22) and highlights her fearsomeness along with her rank as firstborn of Nanna/Sin. The purpose of the composition is openly stated: "I shall praise the queen of battle, Sin's eldest daughter, young Inana."[102] This proclamation is followed by a long monologue by Inana, who explains the circumstances that led her to wage war against Ebih. Because it showed her no respect, Inana prepares for battle.

First, Inana requests permission from An to launch an attack on Ebih, but An appears puzzled, even concerned, about Inana's plan (ll. 62–137). Ebih is a fearsome enemy, and An does not believe Inana will be successful. In typical fashion, Inana ignores his advice and, enraged, disposes of Ebih swiftly (ll. 138–181). The composition ends with praise to Inana for having defeated Ebih, and to Nisaba, goddess of the scribal arts (ll. 182–184).

Interpretations about the meaning of *Inana and Ebih* abound and include the use of the documentary approach that reads in the text an anti-Akkadian sentiment related to Sargonic imperialism.[103] The limitations of this approach have already been discussed.[104] More recently, it has been suggested that *Inana and Ebih* "underscore[s] an essential aspect of the relationship between Inana and her father [=An]—the impulsive, easily angered daughter Inana, and the father, who always gives her what she wants, even when he knows it is unreasonable or destructive."[105] While this is certainly a part of the plot of *Inana and Ebih*, it is not the central element of the composition. Indeed, a better understanding is reached when examining the relationship among *Inana B*, *Inana C*, and *Inana and Ebih*, something which will be explored further in this chapter. And since interpreting *Inana and Ebih* as a commentary in favor of (or against) Sargonic expansionism has been refuted, it is extremely unlikely that Enheduana, who does not appear in the text, was its author.

This overview allows us to reduce the number of Enheduana-related compositions from seven to four. Before turning to Enheduana's relationship with those remaining texts, it is finally time to discuss Old Babylonian Sumerian scribal education.

94 *Enheduana*

The Old Babylonian Sumerian Scribal Curriculum

Most tablets preserving works attributed to Enheduana were produced as part of the Nippur Old Babylonian scribal curriculum in Sumerian.[106] This curriculum is well documented, especially for the nineteenth and eighteenth centuries BCE.[107] Outside of Nippur, Ur, Kish, Sippar, Uruk, and Meturan (mod. Tell Haddad) also have yielded data.[108] No state-sponsored schools existed; rather, education was a private affair, and teachers had a few pupils whom they taught in their own homes.[109] Students and teachers were not Sumerian speakers, as Sumerian had died out as a spoken language towards the end of the third millennium BCE. Instead, they spoke Old Babylonian Akkadian, and a significant portion of what happened in class would have been carried out orally in their native language.[110]

Sumerian grammar must have looked complicated to these Akkadian-speaking students. Whereas Akkadian is a highly inflected Semitic language that distinguishes genders, conjugates verbs, and declines nouns and adjectives, Sumerian has none of these features. It is an agglutinative and ergative language. Verbs are not inflected, but their tense and mood are changed by means of prefixes and suffixes (agglutinative). Furthermore, the subject of intransitive verbs is marked in the same manner as the object of transitive ones (ergative). Finally, Sumerian does not distinguish genders grammatically but separates between person and non-person categories. Sumerian vocabulary is as rich as its grammar is complicated, and memorization through repetition must have been a necessity for students seeking to master it.

To teach Sumerian and the cuneiform writing system, teachers developed a two-stage curriculum similar to that in place already in the Sargonic period (Chapter 3). During the elementary phase, pupils learned how to hold a reed stylus, fashion a tablet, and draw simple signs. Then, they learned Sumerian vocabulary, grammar, syntax, and complex signs. They also practiced simple sentences using personal names and proverbs. The elementary curriculum was conventionalized by tradition, with limited room for pedagogical innovation. During the advanced phase, pupils studied Sumerian literary documents, and teachers designed their own program from a large corpus of compositions.[111] At times, teachers also created their own texts to achieve specific pedagogical goals.

At least in Nippur, two corpora formed a core component of the advanced stage: the Tetrad and the Decad. The Tetrad included four hymns (three to kings of the First Dynasty of Isin and one to Nisaba, the patron deity of scribes), which furthered students' knowledge of Sumerian grammar.[112] The Decad consisted of ten hymns and narrative texts, including *Inana B* and *Inana and Ebih*. Altogether, these might well have been "the *propaedeutical* stage of the study of the great masterpieces that make up the [Old Babylonian Sumerian] canon."[113]

Enheduana the Poetess 95

The compositions included in the Decad were studied in the following (standardized) order: *Shulgi A*, *Lipit-Ishtar A*, the *Song of the Hoe*, *Inana B*, *Enlil A*, the *Kesh Temple Hymn*, *Enki's Journey to Nippur*, *Inana and Ebih*, *Nungal A*, and *Gilgamesh and Huwawa A*. This is evidenced by two Old Babylonian catalogs produced in a curricular setting. Notably, one is *not* from Nippur, suggesting the Decad might have had a life outside this city.[114]

By studying the Decad, students were exposed not just to more complex Sumerian grammar and syntax but also to an array of literary genres. Whereas the Tetrad focused on royal and divine hymnology, the Decad introduced new typologies, for instance, a playful composition about the complexities of the cuneiform script (*Song of the Hoe*) and one of Gilgamesh's adventures.

Thereafter, the sky was the limit, and teachers used whatever material they preferred to further their pupils' education. Thus, one Nippur teacher privileged a group of 14 compositions called the "House F Fourteen" after the place in which they were excavated. This corpus included additional genres, such as didactic texts set in the scribal school and debate poems, the latter pitting two characters against one another in a rhetorical competition.[115] Notably, *Inana C* was one of the House F Fourteen.[116]

The advanced stage of the scribal curriculum was practical *and* ideological. By studying hymns to kings, gods, and temples, narrative compositions about gods and traditional characters, and paradigmatic texts like debate poems and school texts, the pupils—the future intellectual elite, both scribal and priestly—were immersed in the long-established and glorious tradition of Sumerian history and culture. This process was intended "to express the idea of Babylonian unity through the creation of a unified Sumerian Heritage" at a time when this unity had been lost, if it had ever truly existed.[117] In other words, the Sumerian curriculum conveyed an invented tradition created by scholars of the time to distinguish their own scribal class. Differently stated, the purpose of the compositions studied in the advanced stage of the Old Babylonian Sumerian scribal curriculum was twofold. Furthering pupils' knowledge of Sumerian, which had by then died out, was certainly a major concern. Equally important was the creation of an *esprit de corps* among future palace and temple employees.

This scribal class, however, did not operate in a vacuum, nor did it develop an invented tradition simply for its own sake. Rather, it worked at the service of and in concert with the ruling elite. It is not surprising that the compositions studied by Old Babylonian students reflected the aspirational desire of local rulers to achieve the successes of their predecessors. The rulers of Isin and Larsa (and, to a lesser extent Babylon) positioned themselves as the heirs of the Third Dynasty of Ur by deifying themselves, commissioning royal hymns, promulgating law codes, and installing royal daughters to prestigious religious offices.[118] Similarly, the *Sumerian King List*, which had most likely been commissioned by Shulgi of Ur in the twenty-first century BCE, continued to

96 *Enheduana*

be copied in the early Old Babylonian period; the last dynasty in the composition included the kings of Isin.[119]

Traditional characters, "whether divine, legendary, or from (recent) history,"[120] played an important role in communicating this invented tradition. Divine characters included deities like Inana, Utu, and Nanshe, a Sumerian goddess associated with marshlands and the sea.[121] Most famous among human characters was Gilgamesh, a divine yet mortal king of Uruk who became the protagonist of numerous stories written in Sumerian, Akkadian, and Hittite. Worth mentioning are also Dumuzi, Inana's mortal husband, and Enmerkar and Lugalbanda, who governed Uruk before Gilgamesh.[122] Among traditional female characters, notable are Enmebaragesi and Peshtur, Gilgamesh's elder and younger sisters, respectively.[123] Other women, too, might have played a significant role, although information about them is limited (but see below).[124]

Traditional characters are *not* cultural heroes. The latter are widely attested figures in mythologies the world over that provide humanity with cultural hallmarks, such as agriculture, fire, religious practices, and legal traditions.[125] Therefore, most Mesopotamian traditional characters do not also fall into the category of cultural heroes. Exceptions include Enmerkar, who invented cuneiform writing, and Gilgamesh, who, among his many achievements, brought esoteric knowledge back to Uruk.[126]

The use of traditional characters was not limited to Sumerian literary compositions but extended to Akkadian literature. Numerous Akkadian manuscripts pertaining to the deeds of Sargon and Naram-Sin date to the early second millennium BCE. These rulers had become paradigms of kingship—and traditional characters. It is therefore not too far-fetched that Enheduana, too, functioned as one. As such, her historical persona was manipulated by Old Babylonian scribes to serve a specific purpose.[127] She was transformed into an illustrious predecessor whose authority and achievements granted them an additional patina of prestige and perpetuated the notion of a long-ago lost unity—to which she contributed in part by having held her own office for much of the Sargonic Dynasty. In other words, I submit it was her own longevity that contributed to her suitability. She became to the Old Babylonian scribal class what Sin-leqi-unnini represented for first-millennium specialists: a remote ancestor.

Additional evidence for Enheduana's role as a traditional character comes from a related example dating to the Old Babylonian period: Ninshatapada.[128]

The Case of Ninshatapada

According to the extant evidence, Ninshatapada was the daughter of Sin-kashid, king of Uruk (r. c. 1865–1833 BCE), an Amorite ruler.[129] Amorite tribes had played a significant role in Mesopotamian history since the mid-third millennium BCE, and by the early second millennium, Amorite dynasties had been established in the region.[130] Ninshatapada (a Sumerian name

Enheduana the Poetess 97

meaning "Lady chosen in the heart") was not her birth name, which must have been Amorite or Akkadian. She assumed it when she was elevated to the role of **ereš-diŋir** of Lugalirra and Meslamtaea, twin warrior deities often identified with the netherworld god Nergal.[131] Sin-kashid claims to have erected a temple in their honor in Durum (mod. Umm al-Wawiya), not far from Uruk.[132] As for the title **ereš-diŋir**, it has a complex and poorly understood history.[133] By the time Ninshatapada assumed it, the office had become less important than that of high priests and priestesses but was still significant.

Like Enheduana, Ninshatapada was the (alleged) author of a Sumerian work—even though she, too, was an Akkadian speaker. A letter-prayer preserved in the so-called *Correspondence of the Kings of Larsa* is attributed to her. Letter-prayers, or letters of petition, were addressed to deities or deified kings.[134] Ninshatapada addressed hers to the divine Rim-Sin, king of Larsa. The historical circumstances leading to her letter are well known. Early in his reign, Rim-Sin began to annex southern Mesopotamia. Local rulers, including IRnene of Uruk (who was not Sin-kashid's immediate successor, nor a member of his family), attempted to resist.[135] Rim-Sin was ultimately successful in his campaign, and Uruk was incorporated into his territorial possessions.[136]

It is unclear when, why, and how Ninshatapada was deposed as the **ereš-diŋir**-priestess of Meslamtaea in Durum. It might have occurred not long after Rim-Sin's conquest. It is equally possible, however, that it happened earlier, for example when IRnene became king of Uruk. Once her father died, Ninshatapada may have had very few allies.[137]

The letter opens with a hymnic introduction to Rim-Sin, emphasizing his wisdom, magnanimity, and military prowess.[138] Only after 15 lines does Ninshatapada introduce herself:

> (This is what) Ninshatapada, the scribe,
> the [**ereš**]-**diŋir**-priestess of Meslantaea
> and the daughter of Sin-kashid, king of Uruk,
> your servant, says:[139]

The order of her titles is significant—she forefronts her abilities as a scribe before her religious title and her filiation. By establishing a direct connection with a preceding royal line, Ninshatapada might have wished to reassure Rim-Sin that she cared very little about IRnene, the king he had just deposed.

After praising Rim-Sin, Ninshatapada petitions him to be merciful to the people of Uruk, thereby acknowledging his power over them. Then, she asks for her own wellbeing at a time of tremendous suffering. Her plea—and her situation more broadly—fits neatly into the Mesopotamian genre of the pious sufferer, in which the protagonist experiences agonizing hardship and yearns for a return to the status quo.[140] But Ninshatapada's plight is strikingly familiar for another reason: an aging high priestess in an important cult, ignominiously

98 *Enheduana*

ousted from her position by a conquering king.[141] *Inana B* almost certainly served as an inspiration for Ninshatapada's letter-prayer.

Nevertheless, there is a significant difference between Ninshatapada's course of action and Enheduana's. In the latter, Inana was instrumental in ensuring Enheduana's freedom and her return to the position she had held before the Great Revolt. As for Ninshatapada, she requests royal intercession, possibly from the person responsible for her despair. Her exceedingly flattering tone contributes to raising questions about the historical reliability of the letter, which was likely composed by the Larsa court poets to showcase Rim-Sin's qualities.[142]

The tablet distribution of Ninshatapada's letter-prayer speaks to its significance within the Old Babylonian scribal curriculum. It has been found on two tablets from Nippur, one from Meturan, and three of unknown provenance.[143] In addition, it was preserved on an unprovenanced four-sided prism with other poorly preserved letters.[144] Four of them are addressed to the kings of Larsa; the remaining one is part of the so-called *Sumerian Epistolary Miscellany* (SEpM), a collection also used in the scribal curriculum.[145] The SEpM letter is a stern exhortation not to neglect the study of Sumerian, an apt topic for school children.[146] The existence of this prism has been taken as evidence that the 22 letters belonging to SEpM and the letters to the kings of Larsa were studied together, thus situating Ninshatapada's letter within the scribal curriculum. And that makes sense—it is, after all, a text about a scribe. This also explains why this title preceded her religious office and her filiation.

Moreover, by highlighting Rim-Sin's power and reach, Ninshatapada's supplication was useful propaganda for the king as he proceeded to bring unity back to southern Mesopotamia. Ninshatapada's letter recalled Enheduana's plight. Enheduana, in turn, evoked a time long gone when the land had been unified under a single dynasty, whose power was made legitimate not just through divine support but also by means of the exalted deeds of its kings. Moreover, Enheduana's office established continuity from the Sargonic period all the way to the time when Larsa was exerting its control over southern Mesopotamia and when its kings recognized the importance her office continued to hold.

For the rulers of Larsa, the late third-millennium model of kingship was very much needed, and deftly actualized. Warad-Sin and Rim-Sin were the sons of Kudur-mabuk, who in royal inscriptions of the time is called "father of the Amorites."[147] He might have originated from Elam and was never the king of a Mesopotamian realm. However, he succeeded in installing two of his sons, Warad-Sin and Rim-Sin, on the throne of Larsa.[148] Enanedu, who was responsible for major repairs to the **ŋipar** (Chapter 4), was also his daughter.[149] She became high priestess of Nanna/Sin at Ur during Warad-Sin's seventh regnal year. The event was commemorated not just by a year's name but also by a poorly preserved Sumerian inscription uncovered at Ur. In it,

Enheduana the Poetess 99

Enanedu attributes her installation unequivocally to both her father and her brother:

> Kudur-Mabuk, my father, (and) Warad-Sin, my twin brother, [...] I established my residence there. I established my fame forever there as treasure in the mouth of the people.[150]

Indeed, Kudur-Mabuk's direct involvement in his daughter's office is further evidenced by an Akkadian letter he wrote to one Ur-Nanna, which was also uncovered at Ur:

> Speak to Ur-Nanna, this is what Kudur-Mabuk says: I would like to have the copper statue of the high priestess mounted in gold. I will send you Sin-gamil and the (gold) smiths. Please make a decision when you see this sealed (tablet).[151]

Thus, Kudur-Mabuk and Warad-Sin were equally aware of the ideological significance of the office of the high priestess of the moon god at Ur. Rim-Sin must have been, too, and Enanedu continued to perform her duties once Rim-Sin replaced his brother on the throne. This in turn suggests that the Larsa court scribes also understood the importance of Enanedu's office. It is no surprise, then, that compositions like *Inana B*, showcasing Enheduana, one of its most illustrious office holders, remained popular among them and inspired Ninshatapada's letter. This would not have been effective if Enheduana were not a traditional character.

Rim-Sin must have been keen to have his court scholars and scribes embrace his legitimacy. After all, he was a usurper, possibly even the son of Elamites, who, one might remember, had contributed to the fall of the Third Dynasty of Ur! He was also engaged in creating a new territorial state in southern Mesopotamia. As such, it is likely that the composition of Ninshatapada's letter-prayer took place within the Larsa court, wherein scholars used a model they learned in school to convey a new message. Thereafter, scribal masters must have recognized its pedagogical value, considering that they seem to have incorporated it (and other Larsa letter-prayers) into their curriculum.

This discussion weaves several threads together. The letter-prayers addressed to Rim-Sin are attested in the Old Babylonian Sumerian scribal curriculum. Ninshatapada's letter-prayer was one of these documents, and it was likely inspired by *Inana B*, which also belonged to the curriculum. And while Ninshatapada's letter never reached the popularity of *Inana B*—at least as far as the extant number of manuscripts indicates—the two compositions were studied in the same scribal circles for the purpose of promoting southern Mesopotamian unity and an idealized version of kingship. As such:

100 *Enheduana*

[i]f scribal learning was meant in large part as a tool to instruct future bureaucrats and court functionaries in the notion of a common Sumerian heritage, then including material about these two priestesses [in the curriculum] was a logical step.[152]

By considering Ninshatapada and Enheduana together, it emerges that both served as traditional characters within the Old Babylonian scribal curriculum. Ninshatapada's letter presented an idealized version of kingship, to which the rulers of the time strived and to which they would have wanted their court scribes to understand and perpetuate. Enheduana must also be understood as a traditional character and her authorship re-examined through this lens.

Enheduana as Traditional Character

It is my contention that Enheduana did not author the compositions attributed to her. Rather, she was cast as an author by Old Babylonian scribal masters because: (1) she had been an effective instrument in the imperial ambitions of her family; and (2) she was a renowned author—although what language she used is difficult to establish.

Extant evidence indicates that Akkadian stories about Sargon and Naram-Sin were popular during the Old Babylonian period.[153] And while Naram-Sin's portrayal was ambivalent, Sargon was always depicted in a positive light—a beacon of Babylonian unity, ostensibly even its founder. The materiality of his lofty deeds still would have been visible in the steles and inscriptions he'd dedicated and erected throughout Mesopotamia. Those in the Ekur, Enlil's temple in Nippur, were copied and studied by Nippur's scribes.

As a traditional character, Enheduana was compelling because of her pedigree as Sargon's daughter, because of her religious office, and because her life spanned most of the Sargonic Dynasty. These elements provided her with authority as a witness to tumultuous times marked by epochal changes. Furthermore, she must have been an author—or at the very least a renowned scribe and scholar, otherwise it is unlikely she would have been cast in such a role.

The Old Babylonian elite was aware of who she was—the Disk of Enheduana had been ritually buried in the foundations of the ŋipar by Enanatuma, daughter of Ishme-Dagan, in the nineteenth century BCE. Furthermore, the only extant copy of the inscription on the disk also dates to the Old Babylonian period.[154] It was found in a house in Ur that functioned as a scribal school during the nineteenth century,[155] demonstrating that the name of Enheduana was known among at least some scribal masters and their pupils.

How, then, do we understand the compositions attributed to Enheduana? As part of the Old Babylonian Sumerian curriculum, they were intended to foster a sense of cultural unity.[156] The most obvious case of this is the *Temple Hymns*. By "celebrating[s] the greatness of the temples, the gods who live

Enheduana the Poetess 101

there, and the cities in which they stand," the *Temple Hymns* openly conveyed ideas of unity and continuity in content, form, and structure.[157] The *Temple Hymns* has a long compositional history. The presence of a hymn to the temple of the god Ilaba in Agade suggests that the *Temple Hymns* could have originated as early as the Sargonic period, when this god rose to prominence together with his city.[158] In its current format, however, the *Temple Hymns* is better understood in the broader context of Shulgi's ideological reforms,[159] as confirmed by the ninth hymn in praise of his temple at Ur.[160] Similarities with an earlier collection of hymns to gods, the so-called Early Dynastic *Zame Hymns*, further suggest that Shulgi's scholars reordered the *Temple Hymns* to reflect Shulgi's political agenda.[161] This included cultural unity and religious continuity derived from the deities celebrated in the hymns, whose sanctuaries were located all over the south, the north, and even outside the Mesopotamian alluvium.

Thus, the *Temple Hymns* was uniquely suited to reinforce ideas of Babylonian unity. Establishing Enheduana, daughter of Sargon, as its compiler increased its authority. Whether this occurred because Enheduana already was a traditional character, or whether by doing so, Shulgi's scholars made her one is irrelevant. What matters is that her association with the *Temple Hymns* added legitimacy to its message for generations to come.

Inana B, *Inana C*, and *Inana and Ebih* must be considered together. These three hymns (because *Inana and Ebih*, too, is a hymn) are in constant dialogue with one another, highlighting the mastery of Mesopotamian scribes and the richness of Inana's mythical biography.[162] Their interconnectedness is further confirmed by the fact that they are listed together in an Old Babylonian catalog, likely from Nippur.[163] To be sure, one should not overstate the evidence from this catalog, even if it is generally accepted that these documents reflect curricular practices. Yet, at least in one school, *Inana C*, *Inana and Ebih*, and *Inana B* were taught sequentially. Evaluating them in the order provided by the catalog and discussing their ancient titles and their common themes elucidate why Enheduana was associated with them.

Inana C is a celebration of the goddess Inana and her powers, many of which appear contradictory. The hymn's opening line is often translated as "Great-hearted Mistress." This translation is deceptively simple and attempts to render a complex Sumerian verb, **šag₄ gur₄**, which conveys two meanings: "to be wonderful" *and* "to be arrogant."[164] A better translation of the first line of *Inana C* might be "Wonderfully Arrogant Mistress." Or maybe "Arrogantly Wonderful Mistress."

Inana and Ebih also celebrates Inana's powers, although it does so by narrating only her successful battle against Ebih, another deity. The stage is set from the very first line, "Mistress of the Fearsome Divine Powers," arguably an upgrade on Inana's epithet in the opening line of *Inana C*. Inana's fearsomeness is highlighted, as is her rank of first-born daughter of the moon god.[165] When examining *Inana and Ebih* vis-à-vis *Inana C*, one notices the

102 *Enheduana*

narrowing of focus: *Inana C* lists all Inana's powers and refers to several of her deeds; *Inana and Ebih* zeroes in on her warrior-like traits and uses her fight against Ebih as a concrete example.

Inana B further celebrates Inana's awesomeness. The first line sets the tone: "Queen of all Divine Powers." It also indicates a significant shift. Inana's main epithet is no longer **in-nin**, "mistress," as in *Inana C* and *Inana and Ebih*. She is now **nin**, "queen." Oblique references to other myths, about which we know next to nothing, permeate this section, as in *Inana C*. The hymnic introduction makes it clear that Inana is Nanna/Sin's "eldest daughter," as in *Inana and Ebih*.[166]

Even such a cursory examination of these three hymns demonstrates how interconnected they are, drawing upon Inana's vast mythical biography. Indeed, it has been suggested that:

> these hymns belong together and should be regarded as a cycle similar to the collection of temple hymns …. If this is true, the cycle begins with a hymn that strongly asserts that Inana is the most powerful deity in the pantheon. Inanna defies An and wages war against a mountain. The cycle would then end with Inanna coming to Enheduana's aid. Possibly, this collection was meant to communicate the message that Inanna is willing and able to act on behalf of the leader of her temple.[167]

While I concur that *Inana C*, *Inana and Ebih*, and *Inana B* formed a cycle celebrating Inana—and tracking her progressive elevation to the pantheon—it is unlikely that the underlying message of the collection was Inana's willingness to protect her clergy. Even if we accept the premise that she authored these hymns, Enheduana was *not* Inana's high priestess, but Nanna's.

Nevertheless, these compositions are better understood together than apart because of the curricular catalog and the following internal reasons: (1) the thematic similarities they share in celebrating Inana's awe-inspiring nature and powers, culminating in her elevation as the primary goddess of the pantheon; (2) the underlying motif of Inana's conflict with the sky god An; and (3) Inana's status as Nanna/Sin's eldest daughter.

But why Inana? How did the hymns about her help to create and propagate an invented tradition emphasizing ideas about Sumerian unity and continuity? And how did tying them to a long-ago high priestess who served the moon god, and not Inana, further that agenda? Let us consider this in the following terms:

1. the hymns under discussion stress Inana as the first-born child of Nanna, the patron deity of Ur and the Third Dynasty of Ur;[168]
2. the rulers of the Third Dynasty of Ur claimed strong ties with Uruk, whose tutelary deities were Inana and An.[169] These ties were articulated in royal hymnography, for instance in hymns where Shulgi claimed to be the brother of Gilgamesh, ruler of Uruk.[170] Additionally, at least one, but

Enheduana the Poetess 103

possibly more, Sumerian compositions about Gilgamesh were written down at this time;[171]

3. the rulers of the Third Dynasty of Ur emulated the Sargonic kings and carried out funerary offerings in their honor;[172]

4. the rulers of the Third Dynasty of Ur might have carried out a sacred marriage ceremony with Inana.[173] Evidence for this is indirect but compelling, especially when considering that this practice continued under the kings of Isin;[174]

5. the rulers of Isin and Larsa wished to be perceived as the legitimate heirs to the Third Dynasty of Ur. To do so, they continued a series of practices introduced by Ur-Namma and his successors, practices reflected in the Old Babylonian scribal curriculum.[175]

As such, Inana provided political legitimization during a time when local rulers strove to recreate the territorial unifications of the late third millennium. In other words, associating with Inana, who as Ashtar was the patron goddess of the great kingdom of Agade and a deity to whom the rulers of the Third Dynasty of Ur were also linked, granted legitimation to kings whose actual power and influence extended much less than their predecessors'. Putting her front and center in the advanced stage of scribal education permitted the diffusion of an ideal of kingship, which local rulers aspired to, among future temple and palace employees.

But why were these compositions attributed to Enheduana? Ascribing works about Inana to Enheduana connected the Isin and Larsa kings to the Sargonic Dynasty. This allowed local potentates of Amorite origins (or Elamite, in the case of Rim-Sin's family) to compare and associate themselves with Sargon, the founder of the first long-lasting Mesopotamian territorial state.[176]

Equally relevant is the fact that the scribal elite identified directly with Enheduana: like them, she was a skilled, educated individual whose works might have been well known but likely not as relevant to the current political agenda. Thus, Enheduana was a powerful traditional character, albeit one that needed apter works to be effective ideologically.

This is a crucial point: we'd be hard-pressed to argue for Enheduana as a traditional character associated with authorship *if she hadn't authored anything*. After all, even the extraordinary deeds attributed to Sargon and Naram-Sin postmortem were inspired by real and successful expeditions. Likewise, Enheduana became a model for Old Babylonian schools because she was the author of compositions lost to us.

I also believe, although I cannot prove this, that Enheduana's literary production likely occurred in Sumerian *and* Akkadian. I suspect she wrote in Akkadian because its spread as the language of the administration became a tool in the Sargonic imperial arsenal. Enheduana might have participated directly in this process by producing Akkadian works that were

104 *Enheduana*

not incorporated into later curricula. She may also have written in Sumerian because it was the language still in use in the south, where she resided, and provided the Sargonic rulers and their representatives with the legitimacy and authority of antiquity.

Arguing against Enheduana's authorship in no way diminishes her contributions to Mesopotamian cultural history. Indeed, the fact that compositions were attributed to her even if she had not authored them speaks to her influence centuries after her death. Like her father Sargon and her grandnephew Naram-Sin, she became a legendary figure worthy of honor. She was remembered by scholars who reflected, reinterpreted, and reinvisioned one of the most formative times in Mesopotamian history—the Sargonic period.

Notes

1 For *Inana B*, see Zgoll, *Rechstfall*; Helle, *Enheduana*, 7–19. For *Inana C*, see Åke W. Sjöberg, 'in-nin šà-gur₄-ra: A Hymn to the Goddess Inanna by the en-Priestess Enheduanna', *ZA* 65 (1975): 161–253; Helle, *Enheduana*, 27–52.
2 Pascal Attinger, 'Inana et Ebih', *ZA* 88 (1998): 164–95.
3 Åke W. Sjöberg and Eugen Bergmann, 'The Collection of the Sumerian Temple Hymns', in *The Collection of the Sumerian Temple Hymns*, ed. by Åke W. Sjöberg, Eugen Bergmann, and Gene Gragg (Locust Valley, New York: J.J. Augustin, 1969), 3–154; Helle, *Enheduana*, 53–93.
4 Mark Glenn Hall, *A Study of the Sumerian Moon-God, Nanna/Suen* (PhD diss. Philadelphia: University of Pennsylvania, 1985), 764–75; Westenholz, 'Enheduanna', 552–5; Helle, *Enheduana*, 97–8.
5 Ni 13220 (P343573); Westenholz, 'Enheduanna', 555–6; Helle, *Enheduana*, 99–100. Based on paleography, the tablet has been dated to the Third Dynasty of Ur, if not earlier. What survives suggests this was a hymn to Nanna.
6 For an explanation of the change in *Inana B*, see Helle, *Enheduana*, 5.
7 For an excellent summary, see Lorenzo Verderame, 'Autrici e autori nella letteratura sumerica: fonti e studi', *SemRom* XI (2022): 1–54, 15–24.
8 William W. Hallo and Johannes J. van Dijk, *The Exaltation of Inanna* (New Haven/London: Yale University Press, 1968), 1–11. For similar positions, see Sjöberg, 'in-nin šà-gur₄-ra', 161; Sjöberg and Bergmann, 'Sumerian Temple Hymns', 5; Douglas R. Frayne, *The Historical Correlations of the Sumerian Royal Hymns (2400–1900 BC)* (Ph.D. diss., University of Michigan, Ann Arbor, 1981), 22; Benjamin R. Foster, 'Notes on Women in Sargonic Society', in *La Femme dans le Proche-Orient antique*, ed. by Jean-Marie Durand (Paris: Éditions Recherche sur les Civilisations, 1987), 53–61, 53; Foster, *Age of Agade*, 206–8.
9 Verderame, 'Autrici e autori', 15, remarks that "the figure of Enheduanà as a prolific author within the Sumerian tradition has been created by Hallo and Van Dijk [in the critical edition of *Inana B*]" (my translation from the Italian original).
10 Claus Wilcke, 'Der aktuelle Bezug der Sammlung der sumerischen Tempelhymnen und ein Fragment eines Klageliedes', *ZA* 62 (1972): 35–61, 47–8, argued that the ordering of the cities whose temples were celebrated in the *Temple Hymns* reflected Sargon's successful campaigns in southern Mesopotamia, culminating in his victory against Lugalzagesi of Uruk—an explanation that fits nicely with Enheduana's authorship; see also Zgoll, *Rechstfall*, 38–9, for the use of the documentary approach.

Enheduana the Poetess 105

11   E.g., Jerrold S. Cooper, 'Literature and History: The Historical and Political Referents of Sumerian Literary Texts', in *Historiography in the Cuneiform World*, ed. by Tzvi Abusch et al. (Bethesda: CDL Press, 2001), 131–47; Niek Veldhuis, *Religion, Literature, and Scholarship: The Sumerian Composition "Nanše and the Birds", with a Catalogue of Sumerian Bird Names* (Boston/Leiden: Brill, 2004), 40–1.

12   Glassner, 'En-hedu-Ana', 224.

13   Miguel Civil, 'Les limites de l'information textuelle', in *L'archéologie de l'Iraq du début de l'époque néolithique a 333 avant notre ère. Perspectives et limites de l'interprétation anthropologie des documents*, ed. by Marie-Thérèse Barellet (Paris: Editions du Centre National de la Recherche Scientifique, 1980), 225–32, 229.

14   While manuscripts with an interlinear Akkadian translation of *Inana C* exist, the composition was originally in the Sumerian language.

15   Jean-Jacques Glassner, 'Who were the Authors Before Homer in Mesopotamia?' *Diogenes* Vol. 49, Issue 196 (2002): 86–92, 87; Glassner, 'En-hedu-Ana', 229.

16   Piotr Michalowski, 'Sailing to Babylon, Reading the Dark Side of the Moon', in *The Study of the Ancient Near East in the Twenty-First Century. The William Foxwell Albright Centennial Conference*, ed. by Jerrold S. Cooper and Glenn M. Schwartz (Winona Lake, IN: Eisenbrauns, 1996), 177–94, 183–5.

17   Michalowski, 'Sailing to Babylon', 185.

18   Helle, *Enheduana*, 132. But see Gonzalo Rubio, 'The Expression on the Face of the Words', *PBLJ* 10 (2024): 138–42.

19   Helle, *Enheduana*, 132.

20   Konstantopoulos, 'The Many Lives of Enheduana', 57.

21   Konstantopoulos, 'The Many Lives of Enheduana', 62.

22   Szylvia Sövergjártó, 'Originators in the Old Babylonian Sumerian Literary Tradition', *HAR* 3 (2022): 25–47, 38–41.

23   Sövegjártó, 'Originators', 41.

24   Tawny L. Holm, 'Ancient Near Eastern Literature: Genres and Forms', in *A Companion to the Ancient Near East*, ed. by Daniel C. Snell (Malden, MA: Blackwell Publishing, 2006), 269–88.

25   Holm, 'Ancient Near Eastern Literature', 270.

26   Paul Delnero, 'Texts and Performance: The Materiality and Function of the Sumerian Liturgical Corpus', in *Texts and Context: The Circulation and Transmission of Cuneiform Texts in Social Space*, ed. by Paul Delnero and Jacob Lauinger (Berlin/Boston: De Gruyter, 2015), 87–118, 90; Metcalf, 'Sumerian Hymns', 17.

27   These compositions appear together in an Old Babylonian catalog of texts. See Mark Cohen, 'Literary Texts from the Andrews University Archaeological Museum', *RA* 70 (1976): 129–44, 131. This in turn might hint at a mythical biography of Inana articulated along these three compositions and detailing her rise to power.

28   Christopher Metcalf, 'Sumerian Hymns of the Old Babylonian Period', in *The Gods Rich in Praise: Early Greek and Mesopotamian Religious Poetry* (Oxford: Oxford University Press, 2015), 15–49, 17.

29   Dahlia Shehata, 'Sounds from the Divine: Religious Musical Instruments in the Ancient Near East', in *Music in Antiquity: The Near East and the Mediterranean*, ed. by Joan Goodnick Westenholz, Yossi Maurey and Edwin Seroussi (Berlin/ Boston: De Gruyter, 2014), 102–28, 107–8. For the interpretation of **tigi** and **adab** in doxologies as song-labels, see Piotr Michalowski, 'On Some Early Mesopotamian Percussionists', in *Stories Told Around the Fountain. Papers offered to Piotr Bieliński on his 70th Birthday*, ed. by Agnieszka Pieńkowska, Dariusz Szeląg and Iwona Zych (Warsaw: University of Warsaw Press, 2019), 451–76.

106   *Enheduana*

30   This was the case even in compositions where the narrator talks in the first person but never mentions their own name. See, for example, Benjamin R. Foster, 'Authorship in Cuneiform Literature', in *The Cambridge Handbook of Literary Authorship*, ed. by Ingo Berensmeyer, Gert Buelens, and Marysa Demoor (Cambridge: Cambridge University Press, 2019), 13–26, 16–7.

31   E.g., Benjamin R. Foster, 'On Authorship in Akkadian Literature', *AION* 51 (1991): 17–32, 17–8.

32   Martin Worthington, *Principles of Textual Criticism* (Berlin/Boston: De Gruyter, 2016), 41.

33   Brigitte Lion, 'Literacy and Gender', in *The Oxford Handbook of Cuneiform Culture*, ed. by Karen Radner and Eleanor Robson (Oxford: Oxford University Press, 2011), 90–112, 96.

34   Sövergjártó, 'Originators', 27–8.

35   Sara J. Milstein, *Tracking the Master Scribe: Revision Through Introduction in Biblical and Mesopotamian Literature* (Oxford: Oxford University Press, 2016); Worthington, *Principles of Akkadian Textual Criticism*.

36   Sophus Helle, 'What is an Author? Old Answers to a New Question', *MLQ* 80, no. 2 (2019): 113–39, 114.

37   Foster, 'Authorship in Cuneiform Literature', 14–5, 19.

38   Helle, 'What is an Author?', 114.

39   Saana Svärd, 'Female Agency and Authorship in Mesopotamian Texts', *KASKAL* 10 (2013): 269–80.

40   Tonio Mitto, 'A New Edition of the *Catalogue of Texts and Authors*', *KASKAL* 19 (2022): 109–37; Foster, 'Authorship in Cuneiform Literature', 20–2.

41   Dina Katz, 'Ups and Downs in the Career of Enmerkar, King of Uruk', in *Fortune and Misfortune in the Ancient Near East*, ed. by Olga Drewnowska and Małgorzata Sandowicz (Winona Lake, IN: Eisenbrauns, 2017), 201–10; Shlomo Izre'el, *Adapa and the South Wind. Language Has the Power of Life and Death* (Winona Lake, IN: Eisenbrauns, 2001), 1.

42   Sophus Helle, 'A Literary Heritage: Authorship in the Neo-Assyrian Period', *KASKAL* 16 (2019): 349–71.

43   Karel van der Toorn, *Scribal Culture and the Making of the Hebrew Bible* (London: Cambridge University Press, 2007), 44.

44   Glassner, 'Who were the Authors Before Homer in Mesopotamia?', 86–92.

45   Foster, 'Authorship in Cuneiform Literature', 17–8.

46   Besides the compositions about Sargon and Naram-Sin, this category includes the *Cruciform Document of Manishtushu* and the *Agum-kakrime Inscription*. Both were composed to justify a temple's claim to land (van der Toorn, *Scribal Culture*, 34). For royal inscriptions, see Foster, 'Authorship in Cuneiform Literature', 18–9.

47   Westenholz, *Legends*, 34–5.

48   Foster, 'Authorship in Cuneiform Literature', 18.

49   Sövergjártó, 'Originators', 28–9.

50   George, *Babylonian Gilgamesh Epic*, 28–9. By the Late Babylonian period, contemporary scholars had become confused about Sin-leqi-unnini's lifetime. The *Uruk List of Kings and Sage* claims that he was a scholar during the reign of Gilgamesh!

51   *Catalogue*, d+16. See also Mitto, 'A New Edition of the Catalogue of Texts and Authors', 118, 129.

52   George, *Babylonian Gilgamesh Epic*, 29.

53   George, *Babylonian Gilgamesh Epic*, 29.

54   George, *Babylonian Gilgamesh Epic*, 30.

55   Wilfred G. Lambert, 'The Gula Hymn of Bulluṭsa-rabi', *OrNS* 36, no. 2 (1967): 105–32.

Enheduana the Poetess   107

56 *Hymn to Gula*, ll. 197–200; translation slightly adapted after Benjamin R. Foster, *Before the Muses. An Anthology of Akkadian Literature* (Bethesda, MD: CDL Press, 2005), 591.

57 Zsombor J. Földi, 'Bulussa-rabi, Author of the Gula Hymn', *KASKAL* 16 (2019): 81–3, 82.

58 *Catalogue*, d+6–d+8; Mitto, 'A New Edition of the Catalogue of Texts and Authors', 117, 127–8.

59 Földi, 'Bulussa-rabi', 82–3.

60 Földi, 'Bulussa-rabi', 82–3.

61 For a recent edition, see Kynthia Taylor, *The Erra Song: A Religious, Literary and Comparative Analysis* (Ph.D. diss., Harvard University, Cambridge, Massachusetts, 2017); see also Andrew R. George, 'The Poem of Erra and Ishum: A Babylonian Poet's View of War', in *Warfare and Poetry in the Middle East*, ed. by Hugh Kennedy (London: I. B. Tauris, 2013), 39–71, 47–71.

62 *Erra and Ishum*, Tablet V, ll. 42–4; translation after George, 'The Poem of Erra and Ishum', 61.

63 George, 'The Poem of Erra and Ishum', 65.

64 Catalogue, b+2; Mitto, 'A New Edition of the Catalogue of Texts and Authors', 115, 125. This line is heavily reconstructed.

65 *Erra and Ishum*, Tablet V, l. 42.

66 See also Konstantopoulos, 'The Many Lives of Enheduana', 61.

67 Sophus Helle, 'The Birth of the Author: Co-Creating Authorship in Enheduana's *Exaltation*', *Orb. Litt.* 75, no. 2 (2020): 55–72, for a recent examination of Enheduana's contributions as author of this work.

68 Helle, *Enheduana*, 3.

69 *Inana and Enki* is attested on very few tablets, mostly unearthed at Nippur, none of which preserve its beginning or ending. As such, we do not know its ancient title, or whether this, too, was a **za₃-mi₂** composition.

70 *Inana B*, l. 41.

71 *Inana B*, ll. 122–8, 134.

72 Sjöberg, 'in-nin šà-gur₄-ra', 27.

73 Gibson, Hansen, and Zettler, 'Nippur', 549.

74 *Inana C*, ll. 119–20, 123, 137.

75 Helle, *Enheduana*, 21.

76 Inana clashed with Enki in *Inana and Enki*, with An in *Inana and An*, and with Ereshkigal, the queen of the netherworld, in *Inana's Descent to the Netherworld*.

77 *Inana C*, ll. 219–20, 246, 250–3.

78 *Inana C*, l. 109.

79 *Inana C*, l. 14. On more than one occasion, An and Enlil are demoted from their prominent position as the most important gods in the Mesopotamian pantheon. This is quite interesting given the popularity of this composition in the schools of Nippur, the city sacred to Enlil.

80 *Inana C*, l. 271.

81 Wilcke, 'Der aktuelle Bezug', 35–61.

82 A new edition of the *Temple Hymns* is in preparation by Monica Phillips, a graduate student at the University of Chicago.

83 Peeter Espak, 'The Transformation of the Sumerian Temple Hymns', in *Literary Change in Mesopotamia and Routes and Travellers between East and West*, ed. by Rocío Da Riva, Martin Lang and Sebastian Fink (Münster: Zaphon, 2019), 15–22

84 *Temple Hymns*, ll. 543–4.

85 Helle, *Enheduana*, 132; Helle, 'What is an Author?', 113–39.

86 Gwendolyn Leick, *Mesopotamia. The Invention of the City* (London: Penguin Books, 2001), 5–9.

108   *Enheduana*

87   Westenholz, 'Enheduanna', 555 and fn. 53.
88   ISET I 216L, col ii, l. 5'.
89   This is how Westenholz, 'Enheduana', 556, and Helle, *Enheduana*, 99, interpret the line.
90   Verderame, 'Autrici e autori', 14.
91   Verderame, 'Autrici e autori', 14.
92   Westenholz, 'Enheduanna', 550, fn. 52. These are known in modern parlance as *Nanna A*, *Nanna B*, and *Nanna C*. Scholars generally agree that Enheduana did not author these compositions. The one exception is Claus Wilcke, *Kollationen zu den sumerischen literarischen Texten aus Nippur in der Hilprecht-Sammlung Jena* (Berlin: Akademie-Verlag, 1976), 47, who posited that *Nanna B* was also authored by Enheduana.
93   George, *House Most High*, 149.
94   Douglas R. Frayne, *The Ur III Period (2112–2004 BC)* (Toronto/Buffalo/London: The University of Toronto Press, 1997), 31–4. More than 150 objects carry this inscription.
95   Verderame, 'Autrici e autori', 10 and 13–4.
96   Wilcke, *Kollationen*, 47.
97   Westenholz, 'Enheduana', 550–2.
98   *Nanna B*, l. 83. The title is glossed (that is to say, explained by the scribe) as 'Ningal' to indicate that the goddess is meant here.
99   Douglas R. Frayne, *The Historical Correlation of the Sumerian Royal Hymns (2400–1900 BC)* (Ph.D. diss, Yale University, New Haven, 1981), 22–3 and 44–8. See also Zgoll, *Rechtsfall*, 90–1.
100   Paul Delnero, '"Inana and Ebih" and the Scribal Tradition', in *A Common Cultural Heritage: Studies on Mesopotamia and the Biblical World in Honor of Barry L. Eichler*, ed. by Grant Frame et al. (Bethesda, MD: CDL Press, 2011), 123–49, 125–6.
101   Anna Perdibon, 'Nature as Conceived by the Mesopotamians and the Current Anthropological Debate over Animism and Personhood. The Case of Ebih: Mountain, Person and God', *DWJ* 4 (2020): 124–36, 127.
102   *Inana and Ebih*, ll. 23–4.
103   Claus Wilcke, 'Politik im Spiegel der Literatur, Literatur als Mittel der Politik im älteren Babylonien', in *Anfänge politischen Denkens in der Antike*, ed. by Kurt A. Raaflaub (München: Oldenbourg Wissenschaftsverlag, 1993), 29–75; Annette Zgoll, 'Ebeh und andere Gebirge in der politischen Landschaft der Akkadzeit', in *Landscapes: Territories, Frontiers and Horizons in the Ancient Near East. Part II: Geography and Cultural Landscapes*, ed. by Lucio Milano et al. (Padua: Sargon, 2000), 83–90.
104   Delnero, '"Inana and Ebih"', 136 for review and critique.
105   Delnero, '"Inana and Ebih"', 139.
106   Evidence for these hymns from the city of Ur is also abundant, but the Ur scribal curriculum has not been as extensively studied. Nevertheless, there existed differences between the two curricula (Nicole M. Brisch, *Tradition and the Poetics of Innovation: Sumerian Court Literature of the Larsa Dynasty (c. 2003–1763)* [Münster: Ugarit-Verlag, 2007], 118).
107   Piotr Michalowski, 'The Libraries of Babel: Text, Authority, and Tradition in Ancient Mesopotamia', in *Cultural Repertoires: Structure, Function and Dynamics*, ed. by Gillis J. Dorleijn and Herman L. J. Vanstiphout (Leuven: Peeters, 2003), 105–129, 112.
108   Niek Veldhuis, *History of the Cuneiform Lexical Tradition* (Münster: Ugarit-Verlag, 2014), 214.
109   Veldhuis, *Religion, Literature, and Scholarship*, 60–2; Alhena Gadotti and Alexandra Kleinerman, *Elementary Education in Early Second Millennium BCE Babylonia* (University Park, PA: Eisenbrauns, 2021), 21.

Enheduana the Poetess 109

110 Gadotti and Kleinerman, *Elementary Education*, 21, fn. 14.
111 Gadotti and Kleinerman, *Elementary Education*, 21–31.
112 Niek Veldhuis, 'Sumerian Proverbs in their Curricular Context: A Review Article', *JAOS* 120, no. 3 (2000): 383–99. For the Tetrad see Steve Tinney, 'On the Curricular Setting of Sumerian Literature', *Iraq* 61 (1999): 159–72, 162–7.
113 Herman L.J. Vanstiphout, 'The Old Babylonian Literary Canon: Structure, Function and Intention', in *Cultural Repertoires: Structure, Function, and Dynamics*, ed. by Gillis J. Dorleijn and Herman L.J. Vanstiphout (Leuven: Peeters, 2003), 1–28, 16.
114 Veldhuis, *Literature, Religion and Scholarship*, 63. For these catalogs as inventory lists, see Paul Delnero, 'Sumerian Literary Catalogues and the Scribal Curriculum', *ZA* 100 (2010): 32–55.
115 In this case, too, evidence from catalogs is available. See Eleanor Robson, 'The Tablet House: A Scribal School in Old Babylonian Nippur', *RA* 95 (2001): 38–66, 55, and Table 7.
116 Robson, 'The Tablet House', 56, Table 8.
117 Veldhuis, *Religion, Literature, and Scholarship*, 66–80. For challenges to this view, see, e.g., Szilvia Jáka-Sövergjártó, '"Whose Name is Suitable for Songs"– Šulgi in Old Babylonian Cultural Memory', in *Dealing with Antiquity: Past, Present, & Future*, ed. by Walther Sommerfeld (Münster: Ugarit-Verlag, 2020), 243–61.
118 Klaus Wagensonner, 'The Middle East after the Fall of Ur: Isin and Larsa', in *The Oxford History of the Ancient Near East. Volume II: From the End of the Third Millennium BC to the Fall of Babylon*, ed. by Karen Radner, Nadine Moeller, and Daniel T. Potts (Oxford: Oxford University Press, 2022), 190–309, 199–200; Szilvia Jáka-Sövegjártó, 'Stone Mostly Gone: Materiality and Layout of the Ur III and Isin Royal Hymns' Originals', in *The Third Millennium: Studies in Early Mesopotamian and Syria in Honor of Walter Sommerfeld and Manfred Krebernik*, ed. by Ilya Arkhipov, Leonid Kogan and Natalia Koslova (Leiden: Brill, 2020), 310–26.
119 Glassner, *Mesopotamian Chronicles*, 117–26.
120 Veldhuis, *Literature, Religion and Scholarship*, 70.
121 For Nanshe see Veldhuis, *Literature, Religion and Scholarship*, 71.
122 For the legends of the kings of Uruk, see Herman L.J. Vanstiphout, *Epics of Sumerian Kings: The Matter of Aratta* (Atlanta: SBL Press, 2003).
123 Alhena Gadotti, 'The Portrayal of Feminine in Sumerian Literature', *JAOS* 131, no. 1 (2011): 195–206, 199–200.
124 Gadotti, 'Portrayal of Feminine', 200–3.
125 For an overview, see Jerome H. Long, 'Culture Heroes', in *Encyclopedia of Religion*, ed. by Lindsay Jones. Online resource.
126 According to the Sumerian composition the *Death of Gilgamesh*, Meturan Version, ll. 17–8, and the *Epic of Gilgamesh*, Tablet I, 7–8.
127 I already made this argument, albeit in a different context, in Gadotti, 'Portrayal of Feminine', 196–9, and Alhena Gadotti, 'Mesopotamian Women's Cultic Roles in the Late 3rd – Early 2nd Millennia BCE', in *Women in Antiquity: Real Women from Across the Ancient World*, ed. by Stephanie Lynn Budin and Jean Macintosh Turfa (New York: Routledge, 2016), 65–76, 68.
128 Michalowski, 'Sailing to Babylon', 185, also discussed these two women in the same context of authorship, although his approach and concerns were somewhat different.
129 In his inscriptions, he called himself "king of Amnamun," a Yaminite tribe to which the kings of Babylon also belonged. Wagensonner, 'The Middle East after the Fall of Ur', 259. For Sin-kashid and his dynasty, see Wagensonner, 'The Middle East after the Fall of Ur', 257–66.

110 Enheduana

130 Garfinkle, 'Kingdom of Ur', 153–4. An Amorite coalition chased the Elamites away after the fall of Ur (Garfinkle, 'Kingodom of Ur', 161); for the early second millennium, see Wagensonner, 'The Middle East after the Fall of Ur', 202.

131 Wilfred G. Lambert, 'Lugalirra and Meslamtaea', *RlA* 7 (1987–1990): 143–5; Frans A. M. Wiggermann, 'Nergal. A. Philologisch', *RlA* 9 (1999): 212–23, 216–7.

132 RIME 4 4.1.13–14.

133 Piotr Steinkeller, 'On Rulers, Priests, and Sacred Marriage: Tracing the Evolution of Early Sumerian Kingship', in *Priests and officials in the Ancient Near East: Papers of the Second Colloquium on the Ancient Near East: The City and its Life, Held at the Middle Eastern Culture Center in Japan (Mitaka, Tokyo)*, ed. by Kazuko Watanabe (Heidelberg: C. Winter, 1999), 103–37, 120–1; Joan Goodnick Westenholz, 'In the Service of the Gods: The Ministering Clergy', in *The Sumerian World*, ed. by Gwendolyn Leick (New York: Routledge, 2013), 246–74, 261.

134 Brisch, *Tradition and the Poetics of Innovation*, 75, 81–7.

135 The reading of IRnene's name is unclear, and so is the dating and length of his reign. Yet, he governed Uruk towards the latter part of the nineteenth century BCE. See Wagensonner, 'The Middle East after the Fall of Ur', 264 and fn. 310.

136 The conquest and sack of Uruk was celebrated not only by the name of Rim-Sin's 14th regnal year but also in one of Rim-Sin's royal inscriptions (Wagensonner, 'The Middle East after the Fall of Ur', 266).

137 Wagensonner, 'The Middle East after the Fall of Ur', 263.

138 *Ninshatapada to Rim-Sin*, l. 3.

139 *Ninshatapada to Rim-Sin*, ll. 16–9.

140 Brisch, *Tradition and the Poetics of Innovation*, 86–7.

141 Ninshatapada refers to her old age in the letter (l. 39).

142 For a discussion of the Larsa court literature, see Brisch, *Tradition and the Poetics of Innovation*, 37–89. This corpus included royal hymns and letter-prayers.

143 Brisch, *Tradition and the Poetics of Innovation*, 82.

144 Brisch, *Tradition and the Poetics of Innovation*, 78.

145 Alexandra Kleinerman, *Education in Early 2nd Millennium BC Babylonia: The Sumerian Epistolary Miscellany* (Leuven: Brill, 2011).

146 Kleinerman, *Sumerian Epistolary Miscellany*, 45.

147 Wagensonner, 'The Middle East after the Fall of Ur', 274.

148 Wagensonner, 'The Middle East after the Fall of Ur', 274.

149 See also Helle, *Enheduana*, 168.

150 RIME 4.2.13.15, fragment 11; translation slightly adapted after Frayne, *The Old Babylonian Period*, 227.

151 UET 5, 75 (P414979). The letter was uncovered at Ur.

152 Gadotti, 'Portrayal of Feminine', 199.

153 Westenholz, *Legends*, 34–5, 59–60, 78–80, and 95.

154 Enanatuma herself might have commissioned the copying of the disk before she buried it (McHale-Moore, 'The Mystery of Enheduanna's Disk', 74).

155 The tablet was found at no. 7 Quiet Street, rooms 5–6 (Frayne, *Sargonic and Gutian Periods*, 35). For images see: https://www.penn.museum/sites/journal /8972/. For the house and its archives, see Brusasco, 'Family Archives and Social Use of Space in Old Babylonian Houses at Ur', 116–7. For the role of this house as a scribal school, see Andrew R. George, 'In Search of the é.dub.ba.a: the Ancient Mesopotamian School in Literature and Reality', in *"An Experienced Scribes Who Neglects Nothing." Ancient Near Eastern Studies in Honor of Jacob Klein*, ed. by Yitschak Sefati (Bethesda, MD: CDL Press, 2005), 127–37, 130. Among the tablets discovered in these rooms, one also finds copies of Naram-Sin's royal inscriptions, as well as copies of inscriptions by Kudur-Mabuk,

Enheduana the Poetess   111

Warad-Sin, and Rim-Sin (e.g., RIME 4.2.13.7: Frayne, *Old Babylonian Period*, 210–2; RIME 4.2.13.13 and 14: Frayne, *Old Babylonian Period*, 219–24; RIME 4.2.14.15: Frayne, *Old Babylonian Period*, 291–3).

156 It's important to remember that one should shy away from offering a reductive interpretation of Sumerian compositions. Indeed, we should resist the temptation to think that texts (ancient as well as modern) have a singular interpretation—multifacetedness is an intrinsic part of these documents. In the following discussion, however, closer attention will be paid only to their underlying message of Babylonian unity.

157 Helle, *Enheduana*, 53.

158 Manfred Krebernik, 'Ilaba', *RlA* 15 (2016): 392–7.

159 Peeter Espak, *The God Enki in Sumerian Royal Ideology and Mythology* (Wiesbaden: Harrassowitz Verlag, 2015), 57–8.

160 Like Naram-Sin, Shulgi deified himself during his lifetime: Peeter Espak, 'The Transformation of the Sumerian Temple Hymns', in *Literary Change in Mesopotamia and Routes and Travellers between East and West. Proceedings of the 2nd and 3rd Melammu Workshops*, ed. by Rocío Da Riva, Martin Lang and Sebastian Fink (Münster: Zaphon, 2019), 15–22.

161 Espak, 'Transformation', 18–9. For the *Zame Hymns* see Manfred Krebernik and Jan J. W. Lisman, *The Sumerian Zame Hymns from Tell Abū Ṣalābīh* (Münster: Zaphon, 2020).

162 See also Delnero, '"Inana and Ebih"', 134–5.

163 AUAM 73.2402, ll. 1–3. Cohen, 'Literary Texts', 131. Since the catalog lists some of the compositions in the Decad in order, it probably originated from Nippur. Admittedly, issues of grammar, syntax, and lexicon surely also played a role in the determination of curricular order.

164 Fumi Karahashi, *Sumerian Compound Verbs* (Ph.D. diss., University of Pennsylvania, Philadelphia, 2000), 144–8.

165 *Inana and Ebih*, ll. 23–4.

166 *Inana B*, l. 41.

167 Charles Halton and Saana Svärd, *Women's Writing of Ancient Mesopotamia. An Anthology of the Earliest Female Authors* (Cambridge: Cambridge University Press, 2018), 79.

168 Krebernik, 'Mondgott', 368.

169 Margarete van Ess, 'Uruk, B. Archaeologisch', *RlA* 14 (2014–16): 457–87, 460–9 (Eana Complex), 471–8 (An Ziggurat). For the ties between the kings of Ur and the city of Uruk, see Steven J. Garfinkle, 'The Kingdom of Ur', in *The Oxford History of the Ancient Near East. Volume II: From the End of the Third Millennium BC to the Fall of Babylon*, ed. by Karen Radner, Noemi Moeller and Daniel T. Potts (Oxford: Oxford University Press, 2022), 121–89, 127–8.

170 E.g., Jacob Klein, 'Shulgi and Gilgamesh: Two Brother Peers (Shulgi Hymn O)', in *Kramer Anniversary Volume*, ed. by Barry L. Eichler, Jane W. Heimerdinger, and Ake W Sjöberg (Neukirchener Verlag: Neukirchen-Vluyn, 1976), 271–292.

171 George, *Babylonian Gilgamesh Epic*, 7.

172 Foster, *Age of Agade*, 246; Westenholz, *Legends*, 1, fn. 2.

173 Nicole Brisch, 'The Priestess and the King', *JAOS* 126, no. 2 (2006): 161–76, 169–70.

174 E.g., Philip Jones, 'Embracing Inana: Legitimation and Mediation in the Ancient Mesopotamian Sacred Marriage Hymn *Iddin-Dagan A*', *JAOS* 123, no. 2 (2003): 291–302.

175 Garfinkle, 'Kingdom of Ur', 128.

176 The Old Babylonian stories about Sargon and Naram-Sin—in Sumerian and Akkadian—also contributed to this by offering clear guidelines about proper models of idealized kingship.

6 Conclusion

This book presents a new understanding of Enheduana's contributions to the cultural and intellectual history of Mesopotamia during the late third and early second millennia BCE. Rather than focusing solely on her alleged literary works, this study provides a multifaceted portrayal of a woman who otherwise is known primarily as the "world's first author."[1] To be sure, we have very little information about Enheduana's early years—either at the Sargonic court, on military campaigns with her father, or as a student of cuneiform. Indeed, we do not even know whether a royal entourage traveled with Sargon as he campaigned extensively in northern and southern Mesopotamia, nor if his children—let alone his daughters—were trained in the scribal arts. Yet, viewing Enheduana only through the lens of authorship is limiting, as it fails to consider Enheduana's other roles—as a Sargonic royal daughter and as the head of one of the most powerful and prestigious religious offices in southern Mesopotamia.

Enheduana's role as the high priestess of Nanna/Sin at Ur can be reconstructed from contemporary and later sources. Doing so highlights her myriad responsibilities as the head of an institution that was both religious and economic. However, we are left with more questions than answers. Among others, it is unclear how often Enheduana traveled to other sanctuaries or visited her family in their residences. Nothing at all is known about her personal life. The inhabitants of Mesopotamia did not keep diaries. We learn about their more intimate feelings from epistles, and none remain that were sent to or from Enheduana.

The primary role of this book is to situate Enheduana's life *and* the works attributed to her within their broader historical context. This approach demonstrates the discrepancy between the historical Enheduana—the princess and the priestess—for whom we possess contemporary sources, and the literary Enheduana—the poetess—for whom we do not.

Whether or not Enheduana authored the compositions attributed to her, in the minds of the Old Babylonian scribes, Sargon's daughter was an accomplished author and a traditional character to be remembered and revered. This is evidenced by three compositions directly tied to her—the *Temple Hymns*,

DOI: 10.4324/9781032641164-6

Conclusion 113

Inana B, and *Inana C*—and a fourth (*Inana and Ebih*) that might have been understood as Enheduana's, too. Additionally, her only surviving inscription, written on the back of an alabaster disk, was copied during the Old Babylonian period alongside her father's inscriptions. The disk itself was ritually buried in the foundations of the **ŋipar** by one of Enheduana's successors to the office of high priestess of Nanna. This provides additional evidence that her memory and deeds (whatever they might have been) were alive and well in the minds of Old Babylonian scribes and scholars.

As a traditional character, Enheduana functioned as effectively as her father and her grandnephew did. For a few hundred years—possibly as early as the late third millennium BCE, but certainly for the first centuries of the second millennium—she represented authorship and authority in the same way that Sargon and Naram-Sin represented opposing models of kingship.

Yet, her fate was different from theirs—compositions attached to her name were no longer copied after the end of the eighteenth century BCE, while stories about Sargon and Naram-Sin continued to circulate. This should not come as a surprise. Enanedu, Warad-Sin and Rim-Sin's sister, was the last high priestess of Nanna/Sin at Ur before the office fell into disuse. While the circumstances of this event are not entirely clear, around 1763 BCE, Hammurabi, king of Babylon (r. c. 1795–1750 BCE), conquered Larsa and defeated Rim-Sin.[2] There is no evidence that he or his successors continued installing royal daughters to the office Enheduana had once held. Discontinuing this practice likely rendered her—and her memory—irrelevant.

Indeed, Enheduana never reappears in the cuneiform documentation even if her office does. The position of high priestess of the moon god at Ur was ostensibly revived during the late second millennium BCE by the Babylonian king Nebuchadnezzar I (r. c. 1125–1104).[3] It then went dormant for an additional 600 years, until the reign of Nabonidus (r. 556–539 BCE), who elevated one of his daughters to the office.[4] Her birth name is unknown, but Nabonidus tells us that he "named (her) En-nigaldi-Nanna as her (new, official) name and had (her) enter the Egipar."[5] Her name means "The high priestess is (the fulfillment of) the god Nanna's request," since Nabonidus believed that Sin had demanded that she be appointed by means of a lunar eclipse.[6] Nabonidus also rebuilt the traditional abode of the high priestesses for his daughter.[7] Even more noteworthy, Nabonidus claims that,

> I discovered inside it inscription(s) of ancient kings of the past. I (also) discovered an ancient inscribed object of Enanedu, high priestess of Ur, daughter of Kudur-mabuk, sister of Rim-Sin, king of Ur, who had renewed Egipar and restored it[8]

But Nabonidus mentions nothing at all about Enheduana—her alabaster disk lying undisturbed until 1927.

114 *Enheduana*

Ennigaldi-Nanna became the last recorded high priestess of Nanna/Sin at Ur, thereby bookmarking the history of the office with Enheduana, the first one whose name was recorded. Following in the footsteps of her antiquarian father, Ennigaldi-Nanna created the earliest documented public museum in history (c. 530 BCE).[9] This, however, is another story.

Notes

1 For a review of this phenomenon, see Konstantopolous, 'Many Lives of Enheduana', 63–8.
2 Odette Boivin, 'The Kingdom of Babylon and the Kingdom of the Sealand', in *The Oxford History of the Ancient Near East: Volume II: From the End of the Third Millennium BC to the Fall of Babylon*, ed. by Karen Radner, Nadine Moeller and Daniel T. Potts (Oxford: Oxford University Press, 2022), 566–655, 595–7.
3 John P. Nielsen, *The Reign of Nebuchadnezzar I in History and Historical Memory* (New York: Routledge, 2018), 31 and 128. To be sure, information about this is indirect: it is Nabonidus who tells us that he had located a stele by Nebuchadnezzar I depicting a former high priestess of Sin.
4 The bibliography on Nabonidus and his reign is extensive. For this episode, see Michael Jursa, 'The Neo-Babylonian Empire', in *The Oxford History of the Ancient Near East: Volume V: The Age of Persia*, ed. by Karen Radner, Nadine Moeller and Daniel T. Potts (Oxford: Oxford University Press, 2023), 91–173, 125–7.
5 Nabonidus 19, ii, ll. 13–4. Translation after Frauke Weiershäuser and Jamie Novotny with the assistance of Giulia Lentini, *The Royal Inscriptions of Amēl-Marduk (561–560 BCE), Neriglissar (560–556 BCE) and Nabonidus (555-539 BCE), Kings of Babylon* (University Park, PA: Eisenbrauns, 2022), 109.
6 Nabonidus 34: Weiershäuser and Novotny, *Royal Inscriptions*, 165–9.
7 Nabonidus 34, col. i, ll. 39–43.
8 Nabonidus 34, col. i, l. 44 – col. ii, ll. 1–4; translations after Weiershäuser and Novotny, *Royal Inscriptions*, 168.
9 Mark B. Garrison, 'Antiquarianism, Copying, Collecting', in *A Companion to the Archaeology of the Ancient Near East*, ed. by Daniel T. Potts (Malden, MA: Blackwell Publishing Ltd., 2012), 27–47, 44–6 with references.

Index

An 1, 22, 93
Abi-sare 59, 65
Adab 41, 72
Adda 2, 69–70
Adheim River 18
Agade 4, 6–8, 10–11, 15–16, 18–19,
22–4, 26–9, 37–40, 47, 52–3, 61,
82–3, 101, 103
Akkad 2, 10–11
Akkadian: archive 65, 66; language
4–6, 9, 15, 20, 24, 26–9, 36,
40–3, 52–3, 56, 85, 87–8, 90,
94–6, 99, 100, 103
Amar-girid 1, 23
Amar-Suen 66; regnal year 55
Amorite language 41, 96; people
96, 103
Anshan 50
Apishal 29
Aramaic language 4, 87
Ashtar 26, 52–3, 61, 64, 82–4, 103;
Ishtar 18–19, 22–3, 28, 36, 52,
83, 103
Ashur 10, 41
Azupiranu 28

Babylon 10, 65
bal-bal-e 85, 92
Balikh River 16
Bullussa-rabi, ancient author 87–8

*Catalogue of Texts and
Authors* 86–8
Chronicle of the Esagila 29
*Correspondence of the Kings of
Larsa* 97

*Cuthean Legend of Naram-Sin
(=Naram-Sin and the Enemy
Hordes) see* Naram-Sin

dadag 57
Dilmun 26
Diyala Region 5
dub-sar 69
Dudu 16, 26
Dumuzi 56, 64, 96
Durum 97

e$_2$ **ud-gin**$_7$(?) e$_3$-a *see Nanna C*
Eanatum 64
Eanedu 4
Early Dynastic period 4, 8, 15–16,
18, 20, 26, 43, 49–51, 54, 56–7,
59, 64, 72; *Zame Hymns* 101–7
Ebih 93, 101
Ebla 16, 19
Ekur 17, 20, 65, 100
Elam 20–1, 24, 37, 39, 50
Elamite language 39; people 18, 39,
62, 99, 103
en/*entu* 54
Enanatuma 58, 61–3, 66, 100
Enanedu 58, 65–6, 68, 98–9, 113
Enanepada 24, 51
Enheduana 1–4, 6, 9–11, 19–20, 23,
28, 30, 36–43, 47, 50–66, 69–72,
82–6, 88–93, 96–101, 112–14;
her Disk 2–4, 54, 59–63, 69, 100
Enki 89, 92
Enlil 17, 20, 27, 63, 91; his high
priestess 38, 66; his temple 20,
22, 27, 47, 50–1, 65, 92, 100

116   *Index*

Enmenana 24, 38–9, 51, 54
Enmerkar 86, 96
Ennigaldi-Nanna 114
Ennirziana 55
en-priestess 54
Enshakushana 16–19, 50
Epic of Erra see Erra
Epic of Gilgamesh see Gilgamesh
ereš-diŋir 97
Eridu 49; Enki's sanctuary in 92
Erra 88; *Epic of Erra* (*Erra Poem*,
    Erra and Ishum) 88
Erridu-pizir 18, 26
Eshnunna 7, 37, 41
Euphrates River 10, 16–17,
    28, 47–8

First Dynasty of Ur 49–50

Ganunmah 51
Gasur 6, 24, 41
Gilgamesh 95; *Epic of Gilgamesh*
    87; stories about 87, 95–6, 102
gi-rin-na 57
Girsu 6, 16, 41, 64
Great Revolt against Naram-Sin see
    Naram-Sin
gudu$_4$/*pašišu* 59
Gula 87–8
Gutian people 27

Hammurabi 113
Hellenistic period 48
Hieros gamos 56
Hittite language 15; people 28–9

Ilum-palil 2, 69
Inana.ZA.ZA: her temple 3, 37, 61
Inana 1, 27–8, 52, 56, 64, 82–5,
    89–93, 95, 98, 101–3; her temple
    10, 22, 92
Inana and Ebih 3, 82, 85, 89, 92–4,
    101; as **in-nin me huš-a** 3, 82
Inana and Enki 89
Inana B 1, 20, 39, 57, 64, 82–5,
    89–91, 93–4, 98, 99, 101–2, 113;
    as **nin me šar$_2$-ra** 3, 82

Inana C 3, 39, 82–3, 85, 89–91, 93,
    95, 101–2, 113; as **in-nin šag$_4$**
    gur$_4$-ra 3, 82
in-nin me huš-a *see Inana and Ebih*
in-nin šag$_4$ gur$_4$-ra *see Inana C*
Iphur-Kish 1, 23
Iraq 6, 10, 16, 55
Ishme-Dagan 58, 61–2, 100
Ishtar *see* Ashtar
Isin 18, 59, 94–5, 103; Isin-Larsa
    period 3, 59, 61

Kabti-ilani-Marduk 88
Kaku 71
kāṣir kammēšu 88
Kesh Temple Hymn 95
kin$_2$-kin$_2$ 69
kinda 69
The King of Battle 29
kisal-luh 69
Kish 1, 16, 18–19, 22, 27, 37, 41,
    63, 86, 94
Kudur-mabuk 58, 98–9, 113;
    "Father of the Amorite" 98
Kug-Bau 63
Kutha 23, 92

La'ibum 19, 27
Lagash 16, 24, 51, 63, 71, 92
"language of Akkade" 41–2
Larsa 58–9, 65; Larsa Dynasty 83,
    92, 95, 98–9, 103, 113
lu$_2$ zu$_2$ kešed$_2$-da 91
Lugal-Ane 1, 20, 23, 50, 64, 71, 90
Lugalbanda 96
Lugalirra and Meslantaea 97
Lugalzagesi 16–20, 22, 27, 47,
    50, 71

Magan/Makkan 8, 20, 24, 26,
    37, 50–1
Manishtushu 20–2, 24, 36–7, 50; his
    Obelisk 21
Marduk 29, 65
Marhashi/Parhashum 20–1, 24,
    37, 50
Mari 16, 19, 39–41

Index 117

me 92
me-a-am-ra me-e *see Nanna B*
Meluhha 26, 49
Mesopotamia 1–2, 4–5, 7–10,
  15–16, 18, 20, 23–4, 27–9,
  37, 39–41, 47, 49, 52–4, 63,
  66, 71, 73, 87, 97–100, 112;
  Mesopotamian alluvium 18–19
Meturan 94, 98
Moses 28

Nabonidus 18, 113–14
nadītu 65
Nagar 7, 16, 24, 41
Nanna 1, 3, 22–3, 37, 47, 49–50,
  52–4, 57–9, 62, 72, 82–4,
  89–93, 102; his high priestess
  9, 19, 23, 36, 38, 43, 54–6, 62,
  64, 66, 98, 102, 112–14; his
  sanctuary/temple complex 3,
  50–1, 58, 65, 66, 70; his temple
  49–50, 61, 66, 70, 72, 82, 92;
  his *zirru* ('hen') 3, 23, 37,
  54–5, 57, 61, 93
Nanna B 3, 89, 92; as e$_2$ ud-gin$_7$(?)
  e$_3$-a 3
Nanna C 3, 82–3, 85, 89, 92; as
  me-a-am-ra me-e 3
Naram-Sin 1–2, 4, 6, 10, 15, 20–4,
  26–9, 36–40, 43, 50–1, 53–5,
  64–6, 71, 83, 96, 100, 103–4,
  113; *Cuthean Legend of Naram-
  Sin (=Naram-Sin and the Enemy
  Hordes)* 29; Great Revolt 1–2,
  22–3, 28–9, 38–9, 50, 72, 90, 98;
  Great Revolt against Naram-Sin
  2; palace 7; temple 24; *Victory
  Stele* 24
Nebuchadnezzar 113
Neo-Assyrian period 56, 87
Nergal 88, 92, 97
Ningal 57–8, 62, 69, 72, 93; temple
  of 50, 61, 69–70
Ningirsu 64, 92
nin me šar$_2$-ra *see Inana B*
Ninshatapada 96–9
Ninurta 65, 88

Nippur 7, 17, 20, 22, 27, 38, 41, 47,
  50–1, 65–6, 89–95, 98, 100–1
ŋipar (ŋi$_6$-par$_4$)/*gipāru* 3–4, 51,
  58–9, 61–3, 65–6, 68–72, 98, 100

Old Akkadian language 4; period 9
Old Babylonian language 90, 94;
  period 3, 6, 43, 51, 53, 56, 59,
  65, 69, 84–5, 87, 88, 91, 94–100;
  Sumerian scribal curriculum 9,
  84, 89, 93, 95, 98–9, 103
Onion Archive 65–6

Rim-Sin 58, 65, 69, 97–9, 103, 113
Rimush 1, 18, 20–2, 36–7, 50, 71
Romulus and Remus 28

šabra$_2$ 69
šag$_4$ gur$_4$ 101
saŋŋa 65, 70
Sargon 1–4, 6, 10, 15–21, 36–7, 41,
  47, 50, 54–5, 59, 64, 66, 71–2,
  83, 87, 89, 96, 100–1, 103–4,
  112–13
Sargon, the Conquering Hero 29
Sargon and Ur-Zababa 27
Sargon Birth Legend 28, 87
Sargonic Dynasty 1, 4, 18, 27, 38,
  42, 52–3, 96, 100, 103; period
  2, 4–9, 15, 18, 36, 38, 40–2,
  51–3, 56–7, 59, 64–6, 69, 72,
  83, 94, 98, 100, 104; scribal
  curriculum 42
Sennacherib 52
Shamash 22, 24, 39, 53, 65
Shar-kali-sharri 4, 10, 15, 21, 24, 26,
  28, 37, 51, 65–6
Shulgi 55, 66, 95, 101–2
Shumshani 38–9
Shutruk-Nakhunte 47
Shuturul 15, 26
Simat-Ulmash 39
Sin 1, 19, 24, 50, 52, 89, 93, 102
Sin-kashid 97
Sin-leqi-unnini 87, 96
Sippar 22–3, 38–9, 65, 90, 92–3
šir$_3$-gid$_2$-da 85

118 *Index*

šita eš₃ 65
Sumerian Epistolary
  Miscellany 98
Sumerian King List 17–21, 49,
  63, 95
Sumerian language 4–6, 9–10, 15,
  20, 27–9, 36, 39–43, 52, 56–8,
  84–5, 90–6, 101, 103
Sumerian Sargon
  Legend 27–8
Susa 5, 18, 26, 39, 47, 90, 93
Syria 7, 10, 16–17, 29, 55

Taram-Agade 24, 38, 40
TashLULtum 37
Temple Hymns 3, 82–3, 85, 88,
  91–2, 100–2
Third Dynasty of Ur 3, 6, 26–7, 43,
  50, 55–6, 59, 62–3, 66, 69, 72,
  83, 91–2, 95, 99, 102–3; Ur III 4,
  27, 55, 63, 70–1
Tigris River 10, 17–18
Tuta'sharlibbish 37
Tuttanabshum 38, 65

ugula-e₂ 69
Umma 16–17, 41, 71–2
Uqnitum 40
Ur 1–3, 9, 16, 19, 22–4, 28, 36–8,
  40–1, 43, 47–52, 61–2, 64–6, 68,
  71–2, 84, 89–93, 95, 98–100,
  102–3, 112–14; cemetery 2, 7,
  49, 52, 66
Ur-Bau 24, 51
Ur III *see* Third Dynasty of Ur
Urkesh 7, 16, 24, 38–40
Ur-Namma 49, 52, 66, 92, 103
Uruk 1, 10, 16–17, 20, 22–3, 27, 47,
  49–50, 52, 54, 63, 86–7, 90, 92,
  94, 96–7, 102
Ur-Zababa 19, 27
Utu 22, 24, 38–9, 53, 92, 95

Warad-Sin 58, 98–9, 113
Warium 18

za₃-mi₂ 85
ziggurat 52; Ishtar in Agade 19;
  Nanna in Ur 49–50, 60–1, 68, 92

9781032641133